46 Reasons Why Your Cold Calls Fail … and How to Fix Them FAST

BY CORY BRAY AND HILMON SOREY

ISBN-13: 9798564561365

CONTENTS

INTRODUCTION

Hi, it's Hilmon and Cory from ClozeLoop. In the next 30 seconds, we can tell you why we wrote this book; then you can decide if you want to write us a LinkedIn message asking for your money back, or you determine that investing 2 hours to read is worth your time. Is that fair?

> *We wrote this book to help cold callers achieve mastery in their role. The ideal reader uses cold calls to schedule meetings for salespeople who sell products or services to other businesses (B2B). Today, you might be struggling to hit your goals or are anxious about your ability to do so in the future. Or, you might be someone who is exploring a job that requires cold calling and are concerned about how you will find success. Finally, you might be a manager who is exhausted by your team's inability to hit their goals and apply the fundamental skills you know are needed perform. None of these scenarios sound familiar, do they?*

If we're way off base, seriously, send us a LinkedIn message asking for your money back. However, if this elevator pitch struck a chord, let's proceed.

Why Cold Calling Fails

We constantly talk with business leaders who are "trying to figure out outbound sales." While some of these organizations are early-stage start-ups trying to either penetrate an existing market or create a new one, there are also many later-stage companies who have enjoyed success from inbound leads, but now need to scale beyond what their marketing team is able to attract.

Sometimes, veterans in the company will see a lack of outbound performance and beat the "activity" drum, saying that if people were making 100 dials a day, they would be seeing results. While quantity of activity is part of the equation, this book highlights several other challenges that prevent folks from achieving their goals.

The simple truth is that cold calling isn't rocket science. In fact, it's very formulaic, where an organization needs to do the following:

1. Find people to call
2. Call
3. Have conversations
4. Move to the next step or disqualify

However, on the path to performing these simple steps, there are countless places to make errors. We have trained more than ten thousand salespeople and more than a thousand sales managers, and we have listened to thousands of cold calls. Based on our experience with what works and what doesn't, we have framed this book from the position of fails made by callers and guidance on how to fix them. Instead of making calling a science project, when you make a call, scan for these common mistakes and make improvements. That's your formula for success.

Why Cold Call?

For the purpose of this book, the goal of a cold call is to schedule a discovery meeting with a salesperson (also called closer or account executive) who will work with the prospect until they become a customer, decide not to move forward, or are disqualified by the salesperson (figure 0.1). The goal of cold calls is *not* to close a deal.

Figure 0.1: Cold calling in the broader sales process.

If you're in a sales development role (often abbreviated as SDR, BDR, MDR, or LDR), you are likely scheduling this meeting for an account executive or other type of closing salesperson. If you're a "full-cycle salesperson," and are charged with finding your own prospects, then the goal of the cold call is to schedule more time for yourself and the prospect. Or, maybe you're a closing salesperson who is trying to increase pipeline by spending downtime doing some prospecting and make calls to schedule meetings for yourself when an empty block of time on the calendar arises. There are other reasons to cold call, such as to invite someone to an event, but we will just focus on scheduling a discovery meeting.

Cold calling is effective because it goes straight to the prospect who has not converted from other marketing efforts, or they might not have been exposed to them in the first place. Imagine the perfect potential buyer who walked by your tradeshow booth, visited your website, drove by your billboard on the freeway, and still hasn't had a conversation with someone at your company. How can they be converted? A cold call is the most direct tactic.

Optimizing Your Calling Program

To make the most out of cold calls, it's critical to call the right people within the right companies. At a high level, callers have the most success when talking to prospects who fit into their *winning zone*, as shown in figure 0.2. In the winning zone, the sales organization is uniquely positioned to win against the competition when solving specific prospect pain points.

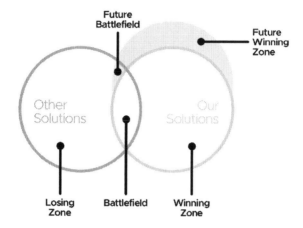

Figure 0.2: Call people who fit into your winning zone.

Beyond knowing who to call, messaging also needs to be developed to cut through the noise. Think about all the noise in your prospect's world from all the vendors hawking their wares to solve problems that may or may not exist. It's hard to stand out.

In our book *Sales Development*, we talked about the day in the life of a prospect, which is included in excerpt 0.3.

Excerpt 0.3: A day in the life of your prospect.

* 6–7:00 a.m.: Wake up and get dressed.
* 7–8:00: Get kids off to school.
* 8–8:30: Commute to work.
* 8:30: Arrive at office, deal with e-mails.
* 8:39: Computer freezes. Restart. GRRRRR...
* 8:46: It's a PC, so we're now back online.
* 9:00: Exec team meeting.
* 9:30: Finance team meeting.
* 10:00: Call with auditors to prepare preaudit.
* 10:20: An analyst found a problem that required Pat to dive in.
* 10:40: Pat preps for 11:00 meeting with the team.
* 10:43: Phone rings. It's you.

Additionally, it's important to create alignment between the senior leaders who are sponsoring the cold calling program and the folks actually making the calls. Expectations typically revolve around the following factors:

Tasks of the Caller: Clearly define what is and is not in the job description for the cold caller. The best organizations focus callers on having conversations and don't make them juggle several tasks that range from research to administrative work instead of talking with prospects.

Activity Levels: Define the activity levels that are reasonable given your technology stack. Most organizations who rely on calls are able to make 20–40 dials per hour with basic "click to dial" technology, but more advanced technology can support higher activity levels.

Connect Rates: After having some experience dialing into your market, identify the rate at which calls will connect to a live human. Segment these connections by gatekeepers and end-prospects to understand how many dials are needed to get a conversation.

Conversion Rates: Identify at what rate connects should convert to scheduled discovery calls.

Calls As Part of a Broader Prospecting Strategy

Calling is one part of a broader outbound prospecting strategy. At a high level, outbound sales is composed of 2 key components: offers and activities.

Offers: What the seller is offering the prospect. Typical offers include written documentation such as white papers or books, digital experiences that include live or recorded videos, or invitations to live events such as a meeting. All offers have perceived value to the person receiving the offer.

Activities: The efforts to reach prospects and present them with offers. Activities occur across a variety of channels, including calls, emails, social networking activity, direct mail, and in-person networking at events.

There is no guarantee that any given offer will attract a prospect when presented through any given channel (email, call, trade show, and so on). The key for a prospecting organization is to have a set of compelling offers that are delivered via a handful of activities and that data is monitored so *offer+activity* combinations that work can receive more focus, while those that don't work well can be deprioritized or shut down.

This book focuses on the calling part of the strategy because it's the one piece that organizations are continuously struggling to get right while spending tons of money and making countless unforced errors. There are endless examples of prospecting emails online, and great books have been written on executing direct mail campaigns (such as Stu Heinecke's *How to Get a Meeting with Anyone*). However, cold calling has not received the right in-depth analysis and tactical guidance.

Should I Hire an External Sales Trainer?

There are countless external sales trainers who will charge your company $5,000–$25,000 a day to come in and teach your team how to cold call. While these folks are often entertaining and deliver many head-nodding points that everyone in the room agrees with, these investments typically result in *enter-trainment*, where the team has a good time, feels a little smarter, and goes back to doing the same exact thing they did the previous week on Monday.

Our goal with this book is to return the power to your company's managers and enablement team by providing the frameworks and content that external consultants use, but with the durability and relevance only possible if the work is done in-house. Spend that money on performance incentives for your teams, professional development programs for your managers, or other initiatives that impact long-term performance.

When deciding if an external sales trainer is a good fit for your organization, consider the following:

Internal vs. External: What exactly does an external entity bring to the table? Good answers include unique expertise and bandwidth, though the price premium for expertise should far outweigh the premium for bandwidth.

Motivation Factor: Sometimes everything that's being done internally is spot-on, but the team needs a little external motivation, and hearing the same words from a different voice often provides a boost to morale. If this is the case, consider a broad range of motivational options because bringing in someone to tell a person how to do their current job better can be useful, but isn't really motivational.

Integration: How well does the material integrate with your existing process? Does the trainer understand your business, or did they do a discovery call and flip over a generic proposal with your logo on it?

Lasting Impact: External training can have a lasting impact if it's reinforced, though these programs are *expensive* to engage with beyond a one-day training and are often overlooked.

The last piece is where companies struggle with external trainers. If you think going external is right for you, go for it. First, try building upon what we have written here. Then evaluate where you can benefit from some help.

How to Use This Book

Our goal is to give you the theory and practical tools to have success-generating pipeline with cold calls. Each chapter includes the following sections:

The Fail: Each title is a mistake that we see cold callers make. If it sounds familiar, dig in! If you don't have this problem, it might still be useful or entertaining to explore what we've observed and ensure that it doesn't become a problem for you in the future.

Symptoms: The signals that indicate the fail is happening. You will notice that symptoms are often repeated, since multiple fails may be tied to the same symptom.

The Context: Additional narrative around the fail, why it matters, and how it fits into the grand scheme of things.

The Solution: Guidance on what to do if the fail exists.

Take Action: Apply the guidance here to your own role. If you have yet to land a cold calling job, pick a company where you want to work and use what you know about them as context to complete these exercises.

As you go through this book, keep the following principle in mind:

Cold callers can only control two things: the quality of their activity and the quantity of their activity.

Each chapter will help you adjust one or both of these levers. Any attempt to circumvent quality and quality and jump straight to outcomes will undoubtedly have negative side effects, so avoid that temptation and focus on the fundamental skills we outline in the following chapters.

We have also included additional resources on our website at ColdCallBook. com.

Let's get started.

SECTION 1: BEFORE THE CALL

1

YOU'RE CALLING THE WRONG COMPANIES

Symptoms:

- Lots of activity with few results.
- Calls are not converting to meetings.
- Message is not resonating with prospects.
- Abrupt dismissal after prospect answers.
- You believe you can sell to "anyone."

The Context: Cold callers who don't understand their company's target market will dial into organizations that will not make good customers. As a result, the cold caller wastes time calling companies where there's no reason for someone to take a meeting; or people do take meetings, but won't end up buying, thereby wasting the salesperson's time.

The target market consists of companies that are best suited to buy a caller's products or services. Figure 1.1 presents an overview of market segmentation from *Sales Playbooks: The Builder's Toolkit*, with the target market consisting of companies that meet values in the *ideal* and *good* columns, with preference given to ideal values. Each attribute is ranked from most important (rank = 1) to least important, to provide more context around where to focus. Any company in the *rejected* column is the wrong company to call.

Note: *While we reference our other books in several chapters, we have intentionally included enough context here so there is no need to buy our other books to understand the topic being discussed.*

Attribute	Rank	Ideal	Good	Rejected
Industry	1	Software	Others	Healthcare
Company Size	2	50–500	10–50, 500–1000	<10, or >1000
Current Solution	3	AlphaCorp	Others	CharlieCo.
Geography	4	US	UK, AUS	Others

Figure 1.1: The target market matrix.

The Solution: Cold calls should only be made into a company's target market.

If your company has a sales enablement team or a manager focused on building sales playbooks, something similar to figure 1.1 should already exist. If not, we have provided an empty table (figure 1.2) below to create your own.

Be careful with the common and more simplistic phrase *"ideal customer profile"* (abbreviated as ICP) that so many sales teams use today. Odds are that your market is robust and dynamic, while an *ideal customer* is simply one data point across that market. What we outlined in figure 1.1 takes slightly more energy to build, but it gives a complete view of the market.

Attribute	Rank	Ideal	Good	Rejected

Figure 1.2: Your market segmentation.

We have also worked with many teams who have different target markets for different products, or even different versions of the same products (such as a basic, professional, and enterprise edition of a company's software). Build out as many market segmentation tables as you need, but don't overcomplicate things. Remember,

Everything should be made as simple as possible, but no simpler.

—Albert Einstein

Once you've defined your target market, ensure that the companies you're calling fit within these values.

Take Action:

- Build out your target market (figure 1.2).

2

YOU'RE CALLING THE WRONG PEOPLE

Symptoms:

- Lots of activity, few results.
- Calls not converting to meetings.
- Message not resonating.
- Abrupt dismissal.
- You believe you can sell to "anyone."

The Context: If the people you're calling don't have pain to be solved, there's no compelling reason for them to invest time speaking with you or your company.

Figure 2.1: Prospects will address pain with high priority and on a short timeline.

Pain is positioned in the upper left of figure 2.1, as finding prospect pain will motivate them to take a meeting with high priority on a short timeline. If the person you call doesn't have pain that your product or service solves, the chances that they will agree to a meeting are slim, and even if they do, it's unlikely that they'll become a customer anytime soon.

The Solution: To ensure that you're calling the right people, first group similar prospect job titles into buyer personas. For example, if your target executive is the head of marketing, this persona will also include people with the titles VP of marketing, head of marketing, and chief marketing officer.

If there is no material difference in how you would market to two different job titles, group them together into a single persona for simplicity.

Figure 2.2 comes from *Sales Playbooks: The Builder's Toolkit* and helps identify the relevant pain points and ways to win with each persona.

Persona	Workflow	Their Pain	How We Win
Head of Marketing	Leads marketing strategy	Misses lead quota Large # of leads are rejected	Can test content effectiveness and double down on best performing content
Content Marketer	Creates digital and print content	Excessive rework	Is able to create more effective content

Figure 2.2: Sample persona overview.

Build out the personas for your organization in figure 2.3, which is also available in the workbook at coldcallbook.com.

Persona	Workflow	Their Pain	How We Win

Figure 2.3: Your personas.

Once the market and personas have been defined, the next step is to find the names of people and their contact information so cold callers can get them on the phone.

Take Action:

- Build out your personas (figure 2.3)

3

YOU DON'T BUILD AND MEASURE RAPPORT

Symptoms:

- Prospects refuse to share their pain points.
- Prospects won't make introductions to other internal stakeholders.
- It's clear that the prospect doesn't trust you.
- Meetings don't hold.

The Context: You've probably heard folks say, "In sales, you need to build rapport with your prospects." We agree, but this guidance doesn't always come with tactical advice on how to actually *do it*. To start, answer the following questions:

- What is rapport?
- Why establish it?
- How do you establish rapport?
- How do you know when you've lost it?
- How do you monitor it?

If you're like most people, by the time you get to the last 2 questions, the answer is "you just do" or "you feel it." That's not good enough. Someone who isn't good at establishing rapport can't be told "you will feel it" and all of a sudden be good at establishing rapport.

The Solution: Understand the science of rapport and practice building and measuring it.

Despite what many have been told, rapport *is not:*

A Relationship: Over the course of your sales career, you will undoubtedly build relationships. However, this person you cold-called isn't coming to your birthday party. They just need to trust you enough to show up to the next meeting, and that doesn't require a relationship.

Chitchat: Senseless chitchat is called rapport in some circles. It's not, and chitchat actually damages rapport if it goes on too long.

Listing Credentials: However much you think you know about your prospect's business, the fact is that they know more than you do.

Let's answer the questions asked in the *context* section above:

What is rapport? Rapport is a level of trust established between a prospect and a salesperson.

Why establish it? Having rapport with a prospect makes it more likely that they will tell the truth. A cold caller who gets open and honest answers from prospects is at a legitimate competitive advantage.

How do you establish rapport? Asking relevant and thoughtful questions is our favorite way to establish rapport.

How do you know when you've lost it? When a prospect stops telling the truth, stops being responsive, and is evasive when responding to asks, rapport has been lost.

How do you measure it? When we work with sales teams, people can often answer each of the questions above, but struggle to provide a good answer to this one. This is where the S.C.A.L.E. framework comes into play.

Measuring Rapport with the S.C.A.L.E. Framework

Dr. David Rock, the author of *Your Brain at Work*, published a paper titled "A Brain-Based Model for Collaborating with and Influencing Others"[1] in *The NeuroLeadership Journal* in 2008. The paper was the result of interviewing over 30 neuroscientists, and the model identifies the approach-avoid response as a means of influence and presents the key "social domains" or "drivers" impacting human behavior.

We have adapted this study to the application of rapport-building in sales using the acronym S.C.A.L.E.: Status, Certainty, Autonomy, Likeness, and Equity (figure 3.1).

> **Note**: Pay close attention here. We will be referencing the S.C.A.L.E. framework throughout this book. You might even want to mark this page so you can come back later to revisit these concepts.

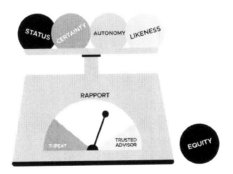

Figure 3.1: S.C.A.L.E. measures rapport.

Status: A prospect's perception of where they are in relation to their peers. When people experience a drop in Status, brain networks light up in the same way as if they have experienced physical pain. A perceived increase in Status lights up networks more significantly than if they have been given a monetary reward. A perceived drop in Status induces a response akin to if individuals have been physically attacked. However, by using a method of discovery and strategic questioning regarding performance or current state, Status increases and the perception of safety ensues. This book will outline question-based techniques rather than making challenging statements in isolation so as to focus on protecting a prospect's Status. A cold caller telling a prospect directly that what they are doing today is wrong will destroy Status.

Certainty: Ambiguity of any kind generates a danger response. Dr. Rock says, "The brain is a certainty-creating machine always trying to predict what is going to happen." Certainty moves people toward reward, so cold callers must let buyers know what is going to happen next. When callers provide clear expectations, they create Certainty, which allays fear and builds confidence. Cold callers do, however, aim to uncover uncertainty in the way the prospect's company is currently doing business. This uncertainty can be used to uncover pain or the opportunity for reward, which will motivate a buyer to effect change.

Autonomy: When people feel they have no choice or control, they are stressed. People need to know they have choices and what those choices are.

Likeness: The brain automatically perceives new people as a threat. Humans naturally feel initial discomfort. Oxytocin response comes from effective rapport-building. Note that it is Likeness that people are striving for here. Likeness enhances the perception of friend versus foe. Rapport actively creates common ground. Relevant customer stories and other types of social proof continue to reinforce the reward perception during cold calls.

Equity: Equitable exchange activates reward circuitry. Unfair exchange activates a danger response. In *How the Mind Works,* neuroscientist Steven Pinker[2] shares that this need for fairness emerged as an evolutionary advantage. In the hunter-gatherer days, when protein sources were unreliable, a large animal might be more than enough meat for an individual, and it could be traded. Obviously, to be an effective trader, one needed to be able to detect deception or broken promises. So equity detection became an evolutionary advantage. In our world, once Equity is achieved, the conversation can be shifted from salesperson to trusted advisor, and the reward triggers begin in the prospect's brain.

Throughout this book, we will continue to reference these five drivers, as they provide the basis upon which a cold caller builds and measures rapport with a prospect.

S.C.A.L.E. During a Cold Call

Now that you've been introduced to S.C.A.L.E., let's look at how it plays out during a cold call:

Status: It's key to uncover a pain point, but not attack the prospect's current solutions. Even if they are not doing what they should be as an organization, if the person you have called has decided to do things that way, their status is at risk.

Certainty: Ensure the prospect knows how long the call will last and what will happen next.

Autonomy: Give the prospect the ability to say "no."

Likeness: Ensure that all customer stories and use cases are relevant to the person on the other end of the line.

Equity: Asks should be equitable. If the prospect is going to give up information and time, what do they get in return?

Once rapport is built, prospects will begin to trust you, and luckily, this process can happen very quickly. Key ways to build rapport include the following:

Ask Good Questions: Demonstrate expertise about a prospect's business through asking insightful and relevant questions. For example, "What impact has the recent embargo with Venezuela had on your supply chain?" is a good question, while "What business risks are you worried about next year?" could imply that the cold caller is fishing and doesn't actually understand the prospect's business.

Leverage Active Listening: While the prospects are talking, practice active listening (discussed in chapter 22). This skill allows the cold caller to control the conversation while getting the prospect to do most of the talking.

These 2 techniques not only build rapport but also help cold callers uncover whether or not the prospect is worth spending time with beyond the first few minutes of a call.

Take Action:

- After each call in the next several days, identify if you positively impacted any S.C.A.L.E. drivers. If you negatively impacted any, identify how to avoid these mistakes in the future.

Note

1   David Rock. "SCARF: A Brain-Based Model for Collaborating with and Influencing Others." *NeuroLeadership Journal* no. 1 (2008), https://www.epa.gov/sites/production/files/2015-09/documents/thurs_georgia_9_10_915_covello.pdf

2   Stephen Pinker. *How the Mind Works* (New York: W. W. Norton & Company, Reissue edition, June 2009).

4

YOU DON'T UNDERSTAND YOUR PROSPECT'S BUSINESS

Symptoms:

- Your questions are perceived as irrelevant by prospects.
- You find it difficult to ask a question that's tailored to the person you're calling, and instead rely on vague and general questions such as "Tell me about your process today."
- Prospects in your target market fail to understand how you can help them.
- You constantly need to ask for help internally to determine how to handle prospect conversations.

The Context: Cold callers who don't understand their prospect's business (at least at a high level) lack credibility when asking questions. The best way that cold callers can build rapport and credibility with prospects is by asking smart questions relevant to the prospect's business and persona. Asking questions that are too general or irrelevant will damage rapport and create doubt that the cold caller can do anything more than waste the prospect's time.

The Solution: Take the quiz in figure 4.1 to identify your current understanding of your prospect's business. If you call into several types of companies, pick one now, and consider revisiting this quiz for each of your market segments.

Question	Disagree	Unsure	Agree
I know (specifically) how my prospects make money.			
I know who buys *my* prospect's product or service.			
I know what each person I call on does all day at work.			
I understand (specifically) how my prospect's life can change after they buy my solution.			
For each persona I call on, I know the concerns they have about taking a meeting with my salesperson.			
I know the alternative solutions (including *do nothing*) that my prospects might have tried other than my product or service.			
I know what would compel a gatekeeper to let me speak to my prospect.			
I know each pain point that prospects in my target market face, that my product or service could solve.			
Each time I make a call, I know a relevant customer story I can tell to my prospect.			
If the person I call isn't the right contact, I know how to effectively ask for an internal referral.			

Figure 4.1: How well do you know your prospect's business?

Obviously, a check mark in the *agree* column is ideal. If you're not there yet, it simply means that you've identified an actionable professional development opportunity. A lot of these items fall into the broad category of *business acumen*, or the understanding of how business works.

The best prospects become customers, which is why we recommend a heavy focus on understanding the business of current successful customers. Here are some tactics to better understand your prospects:

Read Case Studies: Well-written case studies outline the challenge a prospect faced, the solution they purchased, and their results. Within these documents lie great insights into how a company's business operates.

Review Customer Websites: Your customers use their websites to attract their customers; this means these sites must have great clarity around what your customer's business does.

Talk with Customer Success Managers (CSMs): If your company has CSMs or account managers that work with customers post-sale, these folks are a great source of insight into how customer businesses operate.

Talk with Customers: Nothing beats talking with a real customer and understanding how your solution fits into their broader business. Ask your manager if they are willing to facilitate these types of conversations, maybe in the form of a lunch-and-learn.

Review Your Sales Playbook: A well-built sales playbook has a wealth of knowledge about customer and prospect business operations.

Talk with Salespeople: Senior salespeople, especially those who have sold into your market for a while, have a lot they can teach about how the prospect's business operates.

Careful study in the areas above will yield a much better understanding of your prospect's business. Allocate a few hours a week to the tasks above, and you'll be an expert in no time!

Take Action:

- Identify the specific information you should review and people you should speak with in order to get a better understanding of your prospect's business.

5

YOU DON'T KNOW YOUR PROSPECTING MATH

Symptoms:

- Your success varies and is unpredictable.
- When you miss your goals, you don't know if you have a message or activity issue.
- You don't know how many leads or contacts you should call each day, week, and month.
- You don't know how goal attainment correlates to activity.

The Context: Prospecting math provides clarity around how much activity is needed to reach a desired outcome.

The Solution: Define your prospecting math and track it over time. Let's look at the components of prospecting math and discuss common variations and then you can get your own free template at ColdCallBook.com.

First, you need to define your outcome-based goals. Key variables here include the following:

Time Period: Cold calling goals are typically monthly or quarterly.

Desired Outcome: Depending on your company, goals could include meetings scheduled, meetings held, or opportunities accepted by the salesperson.

For example, let's assume that Megan is a cold caller, and she needs to schedule 20 meetings per month. We use prospecting math to determine how many dials per day she needs to make to achieve this goal.

Megan has found that one out of every four people she has a live conversation with accepts a meeting. As a result, she needs to have 80 live conversations in order to schedule 20 meetings.

She looked at historical dial-to-connect data and determined that on average, she needs to make 20 dials to get a live conversation (excluding gatekeepers). Given that she needs 80 live conversations and it takes 20 dials to get 1, she will need to make 1,600 dials per month to achieve her goal.

The upcoming month has 21 business days. Megan divides 1,600 by 21 and finds that she will need to make 76 dials per day to schedule 20 meetings in the month, assuming that historical conversion rates hold. Figure 5.1 outlines Megan's prospecting math.

Metric	Value
Meetings Scheduled Goal	20
Conversations to Get Meeting	4
Total Conversations Required	80 (20 * 4)
Dials to Get Conversation	20
Total Dials Required	1600 (80 * 20)
Days in Month	21
Dials Per Day	76 (1600 / 21)

Figure 5.1: Megan's prospecting math.

What if Megan improved her ability to convert conversations so instead of taking four conversations to get a meeting, it took three? As shown in figure 5.2, instead of having to make 76 dials per day, Megan now only needs to make 57 dials.

Metric	Value
Meetings Scheduled Goal	20
Conversations to Get Meeting	3 (reduced from 4 in figure 5.1)
Total Conversations Required	60 (20 * 3)
Dials to Get Conversation	20
Total Dials Required	1200 (60 * 20)
Days in Month	21
Dials Per Day	57 (1200 / 21)

Figure 5.2: Revised prospecting math with an improved conversion rate.

Multiple versions of prospecting math are available in a free workbook at ColdCallBook.com. If your team's prospecting math is different from what we've built, shoot Cory a note on LinkedIn and we'll add a template to the website that's suited to how your team operates.

Take Action:

- Build out your prospecting math using the resources we have provided online.

6

YOU DON'T RUN EXPERIMENTS

Symptoms:

- You can't identify problems, but you know they exist.
- Your success varies and is unpredictable.
- You don't know if you have a message or an activity issue.
- You are constantly making changes to calling tactics without a clear idea of what will change.
- Your process is unnecessarily complicated.

The Context: We learned about experiments in elementary school science fairs. It turns out that beyond creating lava-flowing volcanoes, experimentation is actually an important business skill.

You likely have learned the scientific method and practiced it throughout high school, college, and even professionally. As a refresher, we have pulled the six steps of the method from K-12 online education provider, Khan Academy:[1]

Step 1: Make an observation.
Step 2: Ask a question.
Step 3: Form a hypothesis, or testable explanation.
Step 4: Make a prediction based on the hypothesis.

Step 5: Test the prediction.

Step 6: Iterate: use the results to make new hypotheses or predictions.

The Solution: Let's walk through a step-by-step example of using the scientific method to improve a cold calling process. First, we start with an observation from a fictional situation:

> **Step 1: Observation**: The data show that meetings scheduled with VPs and CXOs hold at a 65% rate, while meetings with directors and below hold at an 85% rate.

That's interesting. Now ask a question:

> **Step 2: Question**: Why are meetings not holding with VPs and CXOs at a higher rate?

Good question. Now let's state a hypothesis.

> **Step 3: Hypothesis**: I am not uncovering pain that's personally relevant to VPs and CXOs.

Now we need a prediction.

> **Step 4: Prediction**: If I uncover more compelling pain for VPs and CXOs, our meeting will hold at a higher rate. Our expectation is that meeting held rates will rise from 65% to 75% over the course of 4 weeks.

It's now time to design a test.

> **Step 5: Test the Prediction**: Let's work with our sales, customer success, and account management teams to define the most compelling pain points for VPs and CXOs who have bought our

product. These will be used to craft discovery questions that drive the reason and urgency for the meeting we schedule on cold calls. Half of cold callers will use this new intelligence over the next four weeks, while the other half will continue as-is. Results will be compared at the end.

If you remember back to science class, having part of the group do what they have been doing without making any changes is the *control*, while the rest of the folks run the experiment by changing one variable (figure 6.1). Comparison of the results of the two groups leads to higher confidence that the change in the results is because a variable was changed; it was not just happenstance.

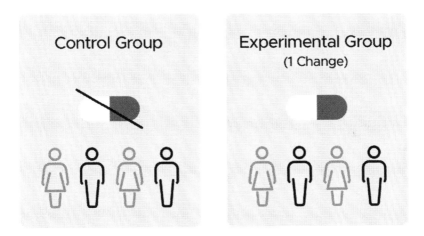

Figure 6.1: Make sure you have a control group when running the experiment.

You might have heard the phrase "correlation does not imply causation." Correlation means there is a relationship or pattern between the values of 2 variables. Causation means that one event causes another event to occur. For example, just because more people answer the phone on Mondays doesn't mean they answer the phone *because* it's Monday. So, there is a correlation among the number of people answering the phone on a Monday. Not causation.

If Pat schedules more meetings when dialing left-handed, the left-handed dial does not *cause* the meetings to be scheduled at a higher rate. Since correlation does not imply causation, it's important to test one variable at a time against a control and determine if the change in results was caused by the change in process.

> **Step 6**: Iterate. Finally, it's time to iterate. Based on the outcome of the experiment, go back to the first step of the scientific method and make an observation, thereby starting all over again. Over time, following this method will build a strong foundation of what works, and allow change only at the specific points where it might positively impact performance. We have summarized these steps in figure 6.2.

Take Action:

- Design and run an experiment to uplevel your cold calling efforts.

Note

1   https://www.khanacademy.org/

7

YOU GET EMOTIONALLY INVOLVED IN OUTCOMES YOU CAN'T CONTROL

Symptoms:

- Negative emotions make it hard to bounce back from rejection.
- You *get mad* at prospects.
- You get mad about things that are out of your control.
- You have to "cool off" frequently between calls.

The Context: Since cold calling ends in rejection more often than not, the caller gets upset that the outcome produced wasn't desired. As a result, the caller changes things that shouldn't be changed and doesn't change things that they should.

Cold callers can only control 2 things:

Quantity of Activity: How much activity do you do?

Quality of Activity: How well do you do it?

Anything else is not directly within your control. Getting upset about things outside of your control is unproductive.

The Solution: Doing prospecting math (chapter 5) helps identify the quantity of activity that needs to be reached. If something needs to change, it can only be impacted at the level of quantity or quality. The key is realizing that doing the right thing will eventually lead to hitting the goals outlined in your prospecting math.

One technique to deal with rejection and spin it into a more positive light is the use of negative goals, which is discussed in chapter 47; it allows the caller to focus on the number of nos instead of yeses.

Frustrated by rejection, cold callers sometimes move away from the quantity and quality of activity that has been proven to work in their organization. This is because even though they do the right things, they don't see the expected results. Then, they start doing poor quality activity or a less-than-expected quantity. If they see positive results after this change, the cycle perpetuates, and eventually, after a short-term blip of positive results surfaces, they see even worse results.

Take Action:

- Whenever negative emotions appear while calling, redirect this energy to improving the quality and/or quantity of your activity.

8

YOU DON'T UNDERSTAND YOUR PRODUCT

Symptoms:

- Prospects tell you they are happy with your competitor.
- Prospects don't understand your differentiation between direct and indirect competitors.
- Your company offers many products and services, but you only focus on those in your comfort zone.

The Context: If you don't know everything your company sells and why, that will hurt your ability to convert prospects on cold calls. Specifically, it's key to understand the following for each product or service:

- What specific *pain points* are solved?
- In which *segments of your target market* (chapter 1)?
- For which *personas* (chapter 2)?

Notice how we didn't mention a thorough understanding of features and functionality here? Since prospects care about solving *their pain*, we direct our energy toward the items in the bullet points above instead of the technical details of the product.

The Solution: To understand the answers to the questions above, we use the *pain finder*, another framework first introduced in *Sales Playbooks: The Builder's Toolkit*, and summarized below in figure 8.1.

Feature	Benefit	Pain Solved?	Persona	Impact	Winning Zone
	Real-time view of performance vs. goal	Missing lead quota	VP Marketing	High	High
Analytics Suite	Alerts on rejected leads	Large # of leads are rejected	VP Marketing	Low	High
	Alerts on possible quality issues	Excessive rework leads to missed deadlines	VP & Content Marketing Manager	Medium	Medium

Figure 8.1: The *pain finder.*

The key for the *pain finder* is to work sequentially from left to right, asking the following questions prior to filling in the column:

Feature: What is the product feature?

Benefit: How does that feature help our customer?

Pain Solved?: What pain would someone have to have today to care about receiving this benefit? Ensure that you identify a true pain point, and not just a symptom such as inefficiency or cost.

Persona: Which persona(s) have this pain?

Impact: What will be the impact on the prospect if this problem is solved? Score on a scale of low to high, or use a 0 (low) – 4 (high) scale if there are lots of items.

Winning Zone: How well is your company positioned to win against the competition (including do nothing or build internally) if this pain is solved? Also score this column on a low-to-high scale.

The *pain finder* is the key to the kingdom when it comes to cold calling. Here's how to make it come to life once it's built:

1. Forget about the features and benefits. These should never be discussed with a prospect during a cold call.
2. Use the *pain solved?* column to craft questions to ask on the cold call. We provide a framework to do so in the next chapter.
3. Use the persona and market segment columns to identify when these pain points are relevant.
4. Prioritize which pain-based discovery questions to ask based on what's high-impact and highly focused in your *winning zone.*

Take Action:

- Complete the *pain finder* (figure 8.1) for your top five features. Hint: work as a team to complete this exercise, as it's a lot of work to get right. Make sure that your pain points are compelling and not simply symptoms such as inefficiency or cost.

SECTION 2: THE CALL

9

YOU DON'T UNCOVER PAIN

Symptoms:

- Lots of activity, little results.
- Calls not converting to meetings.
- Message not resonating.
- Abrupt dismissal.
- Prospects ask for "more information."
- Prospects want to "think it over."
- Prospects don't show up for scheduled meetings.

The Context: Prospects are busy. They have commitments to their boss, peers, and subordinates, and these commitments often require more time than they currently have available. As a result, anything new they take on must solve a significant pain point to get their attention and move up a priority list.

These people have been sold to before, maybe hundreds of times, so the assumption is that taking a call with your salesperson isn't just a call, but they are opting-into a sales process that could require a lot of their time in the coming weeks.

The Solution: Remember the *pain finder* that was first introduced in chapter 8?

Which of the following questions is more compelling?

> **Question 1**: Our analytics suite allows customers to have a real-time view of performance vs. goal and provides alerts on rejected leads. Would you like to learn more about it?

> **Question 2**: I don't know if this is relevant to you, but we've been talking with other marketing VPs who are concerned about missing lead quotas, are anxious about the large number of leads rejected by the sales team, and struggle to hit content deadlines due to excessive rework. None of these are issues for you, are they?

Question 1 talks about a product's features and benefits. The prospect needs to figure out why the heck that stuff even matters to them. It's also a little pushy, with the clear intention of trying to get the prospect to say *yes*.

Question 2 focuses on the pain points that the caller has solved for other people like the prospect (in this case, marketing VPs) instead of focusing on the features and benefits of a product. These pain statements are pulled directly from the *pain finder* (figure 9.1).

Feature	Benefit	Pain Solved?	Persona	Impact	Winning Zone
Analytics Suite	Real-time view of performance vs. goal	Missing lead quota	VP Marketing	High	High
	Alerts on rejected leads	Large # of leads are rejected	VP Marketing	Low	High
	Alerts on possible quality issues	Excessive rework leads to missed deadlines	VP & Content Marketing Manager	Medium	Medium

Figure 9.1: The pain finder.

Question 2 is an example of a pain-based discovery question that was created by using the S.C.A.N. framework that takes a pain statement from the *pain finder* and turns it into a question to ask a prospect. Let's first review the elements of S.C.A.N. and then take a look at how to put it into practice.

Social Proof: Demonstrate that your company has worked with other people like the prospect (Likeness from the S.C.A.L.E. framework, chapter 3).

C.A.U.S.E. an Emotional Reaction: Use words like concerned, anxious, upset, struggling, and exhausted, or other emotional words. It's important to know that companies have problems, people have pain, and pain is emotional.

Assign the Pain Statement: Pull 1–3 relevant pain statements from the *pain finder.*

Neutralize the Response: Get the prospect to opt in by asking a question in the negative form, instead of trying to convince them that they have a problem. The goal is to get the truth, and asking a question in this form is more likely to get them to tell you what's actually happening instead of just providing a "measured yes."

Here is an example of the formula for a S.C.A.N. question:

We're working with <Social Proof> who are <C.A.U.S.E.> with <Assign the Pain>. <Neutralize the Response>?

Putting this formula into practice, the question might sound like the following:

We've been talking with marketing leaders who are concerned with the large number of leads that are rejected by the sales team. That's not happening with your company, is it?

Instead of picking just one pain statement, it's wise to pick up to three, so that the question has a better chance of resonating with the prospect. Remember the original example we gave with three pain statements? Here it is again:

> *We've been talking with other marketing VPs who are concerned about missing lead quotas, are anxious about the large number of leads rejected by the sales team, and struggle to hit content deadlines due to excessive rework. None of these are issues for you, are they?*

By adding multiple pain statements to the question, the cold caller improves the odds that he or she finds something that resonates with the prospect. If there are several pain statements that relate to a specific persona in a market segment, prioritize them by identifying which have the biggest impact and fit most strongly in your winning zone (see the last 2 columns of the *pain finder* in figure 9.1).

Take Action:

- Take the pain statements you built out in your pain finder and build pain-based discovery questions using the S.C.A.N. framework. Practice asking these questions in role plays with peers, and after a few repetitions, try them out with real prospects.

10

PROSPECTS WON'T HEAR YOU OUT

Symptoms:

- Prospects hang up quickly or politely say "no thanks" before you can deliver your elevator pitch.
- Prospects cut you off halfway through your elevator pitch.

The Context: The cold call intro consists of the first few sentences of a cold call where the caller attempts to get the prospect to agree to hear his or her elevator pitch, which is the reason for the call.

When you walk into a store and the clerk says, *"Can I help you find anything?"* what's your typical response? When we pose this question in large workshops, nearly everyone responds *"I'm just looking."* Then, we ask where they learned to say that. Well, it turns out that we've yet to meet someone who went to school or even took a class to help keep retail people away; *they just know.* Likewise, B2B buyers have learned via their environment how to quickly push back on salespeople during cold calls.

If you give the prospect the opportunity to immediately shut down your call, you will never get the opportunity to tell them why you called and pique their interest.

The Solution: While there is no magic intro that always works, your odds go up significantly when you:

Avoid sounding like everyone else.

A client of ours recently raised a large round of venture capital funding and recounted the painful series of cold calls they received that all sounded something like this:

Hi, this is Maximillian from GucciCorp calling to one, congratulate you on your funding, and two, see if you'd be interested in a 30-minute meeting with our product specialist to learn how we've helped other scaling technology companies achieve their goals?

People have been receiving such calls for months, years, and even decades. Just as you can sniff out a salesperson as you walk into a retail store, they can sniff out a B2B cold caller. If you sound the same as the others, they will treat you how they treat the others. And unfortunately, bad callers tend to taint the profession for the rest of us.

Do you think representatives from your prospect's accountant, lawyer, or financial advisor ever call up and say (in a happy-go-lucky voice):

Hey, Marty! This is Dan over at accountingCo. How are you doing today?

No. They don't. The minute the prospect hears this line along with the "smile and dial" tone, they immediately know it's a salesperson and defenses go up (like when the store clerk asks if you need any help).

If you sound different from other cold callers, it will make the prospect think twice about instantly shutting you down. Here is one way to do so:

Prospect*: Hello.*

Caller: Marty, this is Pat with SaaStek. That probably doesn't ring a bell, does it?

Prospect: No. It doesn't.

Caller: It sounds like I've caught you at a bad time.

Prospect: I'm busy, but have a minute. How can I help you?

Caller: In 30 seconds, I can tell you why I called, and then you can decide if we keep talking, is that OK?

The goal here is to get the prospect to either say that they have some time to talk or that they don't. We don't ask, "If it's a good time," because the lack of Certainty around what's going on here typically results in a "no" and an abrupt end to the call. If the prospect says that it is in fact a bad time, ask for a better time with a clear time box like, "When would you have about 90 seconds for a quick question?"

If you skip the first two *caller* lines and go straight to the third, there's a good chance that the prospect's "this is a sales call" alarm goes off and you get shut down before being able to go any further. Each individual word outlined above serves a specific purpose.

The whole point of this part of the call is to set the stage for the elevator pitch, which is covered in the next chapter. Furthermore, by creating certainty with exactly how much time you'll need, the chances that the prospect cuts you off mid-elevator pitch are greatly reduced.

Take Action:

- Figure out a way to sound different from every other cold caller who is trying to schedule meetings with your prospect.

11

YOUR ELEVATOR PITCH ISN'T COMPELLING

Symptoms:

- Prospects say they aren't interested in learning more about why you're calling.
- You can't get past the first minute of your calls.

The Context: The elevator pitch happens after the intro and is where the cold caller describes why he or she is calling.

A compelling elevator pitch motivates the prospect to want to learn more. The pitch isn't meant to close a sale or even book the next meeting, but it should be compelling enough for the prospect to invest a few more minutes exploring if a more in-depth conversation makes sense.

The Solution: Figure 11.1 (which first appeared in chapter 2) shows the three reasons why prospects take sales meetings.

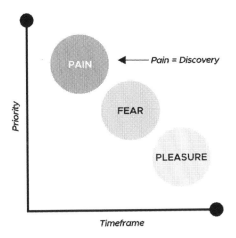

Figure 11.1: Prospect motivation to take sales meetings.

Pain is positioned in the upper-left of figure 11.1, as finding prospect pain will motivate them to take a meeting with high priority on a short timeline. A pain-based elevator pitch sounds like this:

> *At SaasTek, we work with marketing VPs who are concerned about missing lead quotas, anxious about the large number of leads rejected by the sales team, and struggle to hit content deadlines due to excessive rework. None of these are issues for you, are they?*

If yes, then they have pain. If not, that's fine...maybe this isn't a prospect worth meeting with! Notice how this question is the same as what we looked at when applying the S.C.A.N. framework? The best cold callers realize that elevator pitches should have nothing to do with products, features, functionality, or benefits, because these aren't what prospects care about. Prospects care about solving their pain.

Fear is just the anticipation of pain in the future, which is why we draw a circle around them in figure 11.1. Fear is compelling, but not as much as pain.

A reward-based elevator pitch can generate prospect interest, but as shown in figure 11.1, it is lower in priority and has a much longer timeline than a pain-based approach. Here's what a reward-based elevator pitch sounds like:

> *At SaasTek, we help marketers generate more leads and convert them at a higher rate. Does this sound interesting to you?*

What's different between these two pitches? The first one makes it clear what pain points are being solved, with the idea that prospects might self-identify as having these pains. The second, on the other hand, leaves it up to the prospect to figure out how these benefits apply to their world. We have found that prospects who are actually suffering from a pain point will engage in a conversation with a vendor, but busy prospects are reluctant to go through the mental gymnastics required to figure out why someone's product features would be relevant to them.

The key to an effective elevator pitch is to select the best possible pain statements from your *pain finder* (chapter 8). In this context, best means that they are highly relevant to your prospect's persona and market segment, and they have strong scores for both impact and winning zone. We've included the pain finder here as figure 11.2 for quick reference.

Feature	Benefit	Pain Solved?	Persona	Impact	Winning Zone
	Real-time view of performance vs. goal	Missing lead quota	VP Marketing	High	High
Analytics Suite	Alerts on rejected leads	Large # of leads are rejected	VP Marketing	Low	High
	Alerts on possible quality issues	Excessive rework leads to missed deadlines	VP & Content Marketing Manager	Medium	Medium

Figure 11.2: The pain finder.

Why do you think cold callers might be reluctant to use this type of elevator pitch? The most common answer we hear is it's because they're scared that the prospect will say that none of these pain points exist. Well, if a prospect isn't going to buy from us, when do you want to find out? During the first 2 minutes of the first call or after your sales team has invested hours with them to no avail?

The good news is that if a prospect says that the original elevator pitch isn't relevant, that doesn't mean the game is over. Here's an example of a theoretical exchange that gives the cold caller multiple attempts to figure out if there's a reason to schedule a meeting with a salesperson:

> ***Cold Caller***: *At SaasTek, we work with marketing VPs who are concerned about* X, *anxious about* Y, *and struggling with* Z. *None of these are issues for you, are they?*

> ***Prospect***: *We have all of these things under control.*

> ***Cold Caller***: *That's great to hear! Other folks have told me that they're upset about* A, *struggle with* B, *and are concerned about* C. *Do any of these sound familiar?*

> ***Prospect***: *Not right now, honestly.*

> ***Cold Caller***: *Well, it sounds like you're in great shape over there, and we probably can't be of service, unless there's possibly something related to* **(type of work you do)** *that's a priority?*

At this point the cold caller has asked questions that included six high-impact *winning zone* pain points relevant to the prospect, and has also given them the ability to open up about anything else that might be a pain point not posed by the prospect. If there's a reason for the prospect to continue the conversation, the caller is well-positioned to find it.

Take Action:

- Craft a compelling elevator pitch using the framework from this chapter and leveraging the *pain finder*.

12

YOU DON'T CREATE VELOCITY

Symptoms:

- Meetings that are scheduled for closers don't hold.
- Prospects say they want to "think it over."
- Prospects ask you to "send them information."

The Context: During the first prospect conversation, velocity doesn't exist. It must be created. Thinking back to the S.C.A.L.E. framework (chapter 3), prospects have no Certainty around what will happen next or don't feel like they have the Autonomy to say "*no.*" As a result, there is lack of rapport and prospects hesitate to go down a prescribed path due to a lack of trust.

The Solution: We introduced the P.L.A.N. framework in *Triangle Selling*, which is meant to structure meetings and create velocity from one step to the next. Let's take a look at how the P.L.A.N. framework applies to a cold call. Remember during the intro how we said the following:

> **Caller**: *In 30 seconds, I can tell you why I called and then you can decide if we keep talking, is that OK?*

This short sentence is actually the P.L.A.N. for the top of a cold call. This application is the only time in the sales process that the first step (pivot) is skipped since the call is cold. The other three components of P.L.A.N. are clearly covered:

Logistics: *30 seconds*

Agenda: *Tell you why I called*

Next Steps: *You can decide if we keep talking*

A well-delivered P.L.A.N. creates rapport (Certainty and Autonomy from S.C.A.L.E.) and keeps a conversation on track.

At the end of the call, the P.L.A.N. is used again, this time in the form of a Velocity P.L.A.N.

The first step is to *pivot*:

Cold Caller: *(First Name) I appreciate the conversation, and I know I caught you in the middle of your day. It sounds like this is a priority. Would it make some sense to put 30 minutes on the calendar to show how we've helped other [persona]s to solve these issues?*

If the prospect opts into another conversation, the second step in P.L.A.N. is to define the logistics of the next meeting:

Cold Caller: *When would you have 30 minutes to chat with one of my colleagues later this week?*

Prospect: *Thursday at noon central works.*

Cold Caller: *I'll send an invite for a video conference. Anyone else who should attend?*

Prospect: *Just me for the first call.*

At this point, time, attendees, and media have been solved with a couple of quick concise questions. The third step in P.L.A.N. is to set the agenda:

Cold Caller: Based on what you heard today, what are you hoping to get out of the next conversation?

Prospect: Well, I'd really like to learn how the product works for companies like ours.

Cold Caller: We can cover that. Anything else?

Prospect: And pricing. That's it.

Cold Caller: In order to make the conversation relevant, is it going to be OK if my colleague asks you some questions?

Now the agendas have been set. The cold caller has captured specifically what the prospect wants to cover in the meeting and has received permission for the salesperson to ask the prospect questions. Getting permission from the prospect to ask questions allows the salesperson to conduct discovery without the prospect feeling like they are being interrogated, since they have permissions. In the event that a cold caller needs to extend conversations prior to scheduling a meeting for their salesperson, asking the prospect for permissions to ask questions is a key skill to leverage.

Finally, P.L.A.N. is wrapped up by discussing what possible next steps could be coming out of the meeting:

Cold Caller: There are no major decisions to make in the next meeting. Typically coming out of that conversation, you'll either realize that we won't be able to help you, or you can schedule an in-depth product demo. Does that sound reasonable?

That's it! Velocity has been created, and the next meeting is set up nicely for the salesperson.

Take Action:

- Document how P.L.A.N. will be used on your cold calls, and then put it into action.

13

YOUR CALLS HAVE NO STRUCTURE

Symptoms:

- Every call seems stressful.
- You're not sure what will happen next.
- You get flustered when a prospect takes you down an unfamiliar path.
- Your script frequently changes with no fundamental reasoning why.
- You've given up on anything that looks like a script.

The Context: We've seen some pretty ridiculous cold calling scripts Frankensteined together from tips and tricks found on social media or in one-day training workshops. A calling framework outlines the different steps of a cold call and the strategy for each step. Much like a sales process, the idea is to know what to do right now, what happens next, and what must occur in order to move to the next step. As a result, callers always know where they are, can analyze their performance later, and managers can coach to the skills applied to each step.

The Solution: Have a repeatable framework for cold calls.

Step	Purpose
Intro	Grab the prospect's attention.
P.L.A.N.	Ask permission to deliver the elevator pitch in a certain amount of time, and then the prospect can decide to continue the conversation or not.
Elevator Pitch	A short description of the types of pain points you solve for relevant personas in relevant companies. The pitch ends with a question to identify if the prospect has any of these problems.
Reset P.L.A.N.	Ask if the prospect wants to continue the conversation based on what they heard in the elevator pitch, or disqualify.
Qualification	Ask questions to determine if they're qualified to be sent to a salesperson.
Velocity P.L.A.N.	Schedule the meeting with the salesperson, or disqualify.

Figure 13.1: Sample cold call framework.

Figure 13.1 shows one option for a calling framework. There are many effective ways to structure a call so that it doesn't have to look like this exactly; just ensure that you have a strong framework backed by sound theory.

Let's look at the transcript of a call that was made using the framework in figure 13.1 through three lenses: the caller, the prospect, and the OmniView.

The OmniView is the most important of these three lenses. Think of this view as a drone hovering above the conversation, observing how the call is progressing, and reporting feedback to the caller. Developing the ability to view conversations through this lens is essential. It allows cold callers to be emotionally detached from outcomes and leads them to focus on cold call fundamentals.

Prospect: Hello.

Caller: *Marty, this is Pat with SaaStek. That probably doesn't ring a bell, does it?*

OmniView: By asking this question, we force the prospect to think about if they know you or your company, and respond. If the answer is yes, a logical response is to ask what they know, and then proceed. This opening statement, combined with what the caller will say next, sounds different from what most smile-and-dial cold callers say, such as asking "How are you doing today?" in a cheery voice. Our goal is to throw the prospect off a little bit so they are open to hearing what we have to say instead of shutting us out when they realize that it's a cold call.

Prospect: No. It doesn't.

Caller: It sounds like I've caught you at a bad time.

Prospect: I'm busy, but have a minute. How can I help you?

OmniView: The goal here is to get the prospect to say that they have some time to talk. In this framework we don't ask if it's a good time because the lack of Certainty typically results in a "no" and an abrupt end to the call. If the prospect says that it is in fact a bad time, ask for a better time with a clear time box like, "When would you have about 90 seconds for a quick question?"

Caller: In 30 seconds, I can tell you why I called, and then you can decide if we keep talking, is that OK?

Prospect: Sure.

OmniView: By asking for a specific amount of time, the caller has created Certainty (from S.C.A.L.E.) with the prospect. Just be sure to ask for the amount of time you need.

Caller: We're working with other marketing leaders who are concerned about _____, anxious about _____, and struggle with _____. None of these are happening at your company, are they?

OmniView: The caller used the S.C.A.N. framework (chapter 9) to identify pain. They focused on pain points that are most relevant to the prospect's persona, market segment, and anything else known about them. The caller also has backup pain points to discuss if none of these land. Notice how the product or service offered is not discussed.

> *Prospect: I gotta tell you. We just had a meeting about _____, big problem over here, so it's kind of weird that you called.*

> *Caller: Sorry to hear that. If you're interested, I can set up some time with one of our product specialists who can talk about how we've solved similar problems for other customers in the (INDUSTRY) before. Would that be something you'd like to explore?*

OmniView: The caller empathizes with the prospect and then pivots to close, leveraging relevant messaging along the way.

> *Prospect: Yeah, that sounds good. I'm free later this week, if we keep it short.*

> *Caller: We can keep it short. Before we book the meeting, is it OK if I ask three more questions to get you to the right person on my team?*

OmniView: This caller's manager requires them to obtain some qualification information from the prospect before passing the lead. Before doing so, the caller asks permission to ask a specific number of questions to create Certainty with the prospect. Notice how the caller is simply resetting the P.L.A.N. to adjust the agenda (ask three questions) and next steps (will book the meeting). The key is that there is always an active agenda and possible next steps that the prospect has agreed to.

> *Prospect: Sure.*

> *Caller: My notes show that you're a 1,200-person company headquartered in Denver. Is that right?*

Prospect: Yes.

Caller: And do you use Salesforce.com?

Prospect: We do.

Caller: Thanks. And finally, is there anyone else on your team who you think might be interested in joining this call?

Prospect: Bob is our VP of product marketing. I'll invite him, and if he's not free, he'll catch us next time.

OmniView: Notice the efficiency and professionalism here? No long irrelevant stories. No pushing of product or introducing case studies.

Caller: Sounds good. What times work for you Thursday or Friday for half an hour?

Prospect: Thursday after two, mountain time.

Caller: I'm sending an invite for three. Can you go ahead and accept it so that I know you received it? You'll be meeting with my colleague Sarah. She'll be happy to talk a little about what we do. Usually to make sure that she makes things relevant to you, she likes to ask a few questions first, will that be OK?

Prospect: Of course.

Caller: Sounds good. There won't be any big decisions to make in that meeting. You'll either realize that we can't help, and that's OK. Or, if it looks like there's an opportunity to work together, Sarah will work with you to schedule a product demo. Does that work?

OmniView: The caller just executed a Velocity Plan (chapter 12) to keep momentum going into the next meeting.

Prospect: *Sounds good.*

Caller: *That's all I have. Expect that invite shortly.*

Prospect: *Thanks!*

This is what happens when a caller catches a prospect who has pain and is willing to talk. In chapter 15, we will begin to explore what happens if the call doesn't go as smoothly as it did here.

Take Action:

- Build out a cold calling framework for you to use based on the template provided in this chapter.

14

YOU DON'T "WATCH FILM"

Symptoms:

- You don't listen to recorded calls to identify areas for improvement.
- You don't ask your manager for feedback on recorded calls.

The Context: The best athletes in the world watch their game film every week. The best chess players review their matches. And, the best cold callers listen to their conversations with prospects to understand what they could have done better.

The Solution: Once your calls have structure (chapter 13), you can create a structured rubric to grade your calls and seek feedback from others. Record your cold calls and listen to multiple calls each week in order to identify areas for improvement. Ask your manager to do the same.

The key to reviewing a call is to have a rubric, such as the one in figure 14.1. It's best to keep scoring simple, using zero points for "didn't do it," one point for "did it," and two points for "did it well."

Component	Cold Caller		Manager	
	Score	Notes	Score	Notes
Intro	1		1	
P.L.A.N.	1		0	Did not complete
Elevator Pitch	2	I think I nailed it	2	Highly relevant!
Pain	1		2	Very strong!
Resistance	2		2	Solid technique
Next Steps	1		1	
Rapport	1		1	
Questions	1	Felt like I could have improved	1	Let's discuss; opportunity here

Figure 14.1: Cold call review rubric.

Callers should always score their own work, and then have managers score some of them as well. Discrepancies are a good point for conversation.

We're aware that different states have different laws about call recording. Work with your manager to sort out how you can get your calls recorded and start analyzing your own conversations and getting actionable feedback from others.

Regardless of any recording law, we don't know of anywhere that it's illegal for a cold caller to sit a recording device on their desk and capture their side of the conversation. This less-than-perfect solution still helps identify improvement opportunities, so try this idea if your company won't let you record two-way conversations with prospects.

Take Action:

- Record your calls and listen to several calls a week to identify areas for improvement. If you don't already score your own calls against a rubric, build a rubric using figure 14.1 and start scoring them!

15

YOU DON'T UNDERSTAND WHAT
RESISTANCE IS

Symptoms:

- Prospects don't want to move forward with a meeting, and you don't know why.
- Your *objection handling* techniques are not working.
- Calls frequently end with a request to send information and no commitment to take a meeting.

The Context: Example conversations in the previous few chapters assume that no Resistance is presented by the prospect. However, Resistance is frequent in cold calls, so it's important to understand what it is and how to manage it.

We find that performance is improved when callers stop viewing Resistance as "an objection that needs to be handled," and start seeing it as "an invitation to have a conversation."

The Solution: In this chapter, we will review the three types of Resistance that we originally published in *Triangle Selling*.

In his book, *Resistance and Persuasion*, Dr. Eric Knowles identifies only three types of Resistance:[1] Reactance, Skepticism and Inertia.

Reactance
Reactance is resistance to the sales process itself. It's that stubborn kid in all of us who says, "I will not be sold!" "I don't have to do this!" "I know what you're up to, Salesperson!" These examples demonstrate the appearance of the Autonomy driver of S.C.A.L.E.

Here is an example of reactance that would appear near the beginning of a cold call:

I'm busy and don't have time to explore new solutions.

At the top of a call, the prospect has very little idea about what you do or if you can really help solve any of their problems. They are simply pushing back because they don't want to enter a sales process.

Skepticism
This type of Resistance is what salespeople are likely most accustomed to and where traditional sales training channels its energy. Prospects are suspicious of sellers, their products, and their companies. Caveat emptor (buyer beware) and the anticipation of regret are topics of discussion during the prospect's internal meetings. These examples show the Certainty driver of S.C.A.L.E. rearing its head. Skepticism is Resistance against the offer. It has to do with the specific value (including features and benefits) of what is being sold.

Here is an example of skepticism:

Who else have you worked with in our industry, what did you do for them, and what results did they see?

Inertia

Wikipedia says, "Inertia is the resistance of any physical object to a change in its state of motion or rest, or the tendency of an object to resist any change in its motion." This form of Resistance is the biggest challenge a salesperson will face. Self-preservation has paralyzed the prospect. This person does nothing, possibly because past failures and disappointments are replaying over and over in their mind. Or they might believe that they already own or understand what they're being sold. Status and the perception of the current state being "just fine" are at work here.

Here is an example of inertia-related Resistance:

> *Sure, it's an issue. We have the end of the quarter coming up and then our big revenue push into the end of the year. Maybe we could revisit this conversation in a few months?*

Categorizing Your Resistance

Figure 15.1 allows you to categorize Resistance you face as reactance, skepticism, or inertia.

Prospect Resistance	Type (Reactance, Skepticism, or Inertia)
I don't have time to talk	*Reactance*
It doesn't seem relevant to us	*Skepticism*
We don't want to change systems	*Inertia*

Figure 15.1: Categorize Resistance.

In chapter 16, we will further explore how to manage Resistance.

Take Action:

- Complete figure 15.1 to include common Resistance you encounter and categorize it.

Note

1. Eric Knowles, Jay A. Linn. "Resistance and Persuasion." Psychology Press, December 2003.

16

YOU'RE BUSY *HANDLING OBJECTIONS*

Symptoms:

- Your responses to objections are defensive.
- When met with an objection, you don't ask a question or use active listening.
- You use the ineffective "feel, felt, found" framework, which is a long-winded way of trying to convince a prospect of something.
- Calls frequently end with a request to send information and no commitment to take a meeting.

The Context: Poor Resistance management will damage rapport. Defensive and self-promotional responses to prospect Resistance (objections) are not well received by prospects who are eager to get off the phone. Great Resistance management will create the velocity needed to put a meeting on the calendar with a salesperson and get credit for creating an opportunity, or will lead to quick disqualification.

The Solution: If you want to get a fast start on Resistance management, here is an easy framework to use:

Validate: Demonstrate that what the prospect said is a valid concern.

Get Permission: Ask permission to ask a question to clarify the Resistance.

Ask a Question: Ask your question!

Here's an example of this framework in action:

Prospect: I don't think we can buy unless your data can automatically populate into our executive dashboards.

Caller: That's a valid concern. Can I ask a question about that?

Prospect: Sure.

Caller: How are you integrating this data automatically today?

The caller validated and asked permission to ask a question, and then asked. The question here would work well if the caller suspected, based upon what they know about how most companies integrate their data, that the current state did not include automated data.

In some cases, the validation and permission steps can be skipped, so the caller can jump straight to the question. Any question that could damage rapport if it is asked directly (damage Status, for example) should be preceded with permission to ask a question. The risk of negatively impacting Status is mitigated by asking permission, but if the caller can respond conversationally, skipping straight to the question is fine, as shown here:

Prospect: We are really price conscious over here.

Caller: It sounds like a price point of ten-to-twenty thousand a year would be out of the question then. Is that the case?

This *disqualifying question* allows the caller to get the truth. If the prospect agrees with the statement, the caller can either go back to uncovering pain that might justify a $10K–20k spend, or disqualify this prospect and move on.

And, of course, when it comes to managing Resistance, *never be defensive*. Defensive responses to Resistance create a hostile environment with a prospect. The best cold callers we work with realize that when they hear Resistance, it's not necessarily a problem but rather an invitation to have a conversation about something the prospect wishes to explore.

Take Action:

- Write down how you would apply this framework to your three most common objections, role play a few times with a colleague, and then put this learning into action on live cold calls.

17

YOU TALK ABOUT YOUR PRODUCT AND COMPANY INSTEAD OF LOOKING FOR PAIN

Symptoms:

- Lots of activity with few results.
- Calls not converting to meetings.
- Message not resonating.
- Abrupt dismissal.
- Prospects ask you to "send information."

The Context: When a prospect hears about a product feature, their mind immediately starts to ask, "Why would this feature matter to me?" Sometimes the mental leap needed to figure out why a product or company is interesting is simple to make, though not always. The more the energy required for a prospect to understand why they should care, the lower your conversion rates will be.

The Solution: If someone asked you on a call, "What does your company do," how would you respond? We typically hear four categories of responses to this question:

> **Product-Focused**: We are an AI-enabled SaasTek product that leverages the latest technology to help marketers produce more leads, faster.

Company-Focused: We spun out of the Stanford high-tech innovation labs and are led by 2 veteran founders who have three exits between the two of them and have raised over $300MM in venture capital funding. They're really smart.

Customer-Focused: We work with big companies like General Motors, Hilton Hotels, and Google.

Pain-Focused: We work with marketing VPs who are concerned about missing lead quotas, are anxious about the large number of leads rejected by the sales team, and struggle to hit content deadlines due to excessive rework.

Figure 17.1 outlines how folks respond to each of these four approaches.

Focus	Prospect Response
Product	"I don't know what that means."
Company	"That's cool, I guess...I know smart people too."
Customer	Option 1: "Some of those are relevant to me."
	Option 2: "None of those companies are like mine."
Pain	Option 1: "I have that pain."
	Option 2: "I don't have that pain."

Figure 17.1: Responses to product, company, and customer focuses.

Why make the prospect work hard to figure out why they should speak with you or risk damaging rapport (Likeness from S.C.A.L.E.) when you can make it really easy for them to understand how you might be able to help?

Instead of talking about the product and *hoping* that the prospect can tell you a pain point they have...

Prospect: *What are some of the new features you've released?*

Cold Caller: Our new CRM API is live. Would you like to schedule a conversation to learn more?

. . . try using a pain-based discovery question instead.

Prospect: What are some of the new features you've released?

Cold Caller: We just had a new product release to help folks who are struggling to reconcile data between their CRM and accounting software. Would you like to schedule a conversation to learn more?

If the prospect is struggling to reconcile data between their CRM and accounting software, do you think they'll take a meeting? As long as it's a priority for the person being called, they likely will. They aren't necessarily buying yet, but they'll invest some time to learn more.

What if they aren't struggling to reconcile data between their CRM and accounting software? Well, they probably won't take a meeting. Guess what else they won't do? They won't get deep into a sales process and "go dark" because there was never a real problem to solve in the first place.

Cold callers are often intimidated by asking pain-based discovery questions since they are scared that a prospect will say "no." The goal of cold calling isn't to get someone to buy, but rather to uncover a reason that a prospect might want to have another conversation. Even if the prospect says "no" to this initial question, that doesn't mean that they can't ask another. Imagine in this case that the person being called is the director of sales operations at a fast-growing technology company.

Cold Caller: We just had a new product release to help folks struggling to reconcile data between their CRM and accounting software. Would you like to schedule a conversation to learn more?

Prospect: No, that's not relevant to me.

Cold Caller: We've also helped folks who are anxious about getting sales commission payments right and are concerned that their salespeople are discounting too much. You're not seeing any of these issues, are you?

This persistence around pain-based messaging allows the cold caller to do their best to uncover a pain point that is compelling enough to get the next meeting on the calendar or to disqualify quickly.

Take Action:

- Listen to three of your recorded calls and identify where you could have replaced conversation about features with pain-based messaging.

18

YOUR CUSTOMER STORIES ARE
IRRELEVANT TO YOUR PROSPECT

Symptoms:

- Lots of activity, little results.
- Calls not converting to meetings.
- Message not resonating.
- Abrupt dismissal.
- Prospect says, "Send me information."

The Context: When a prospect hears a story about how the cold caller's company has helped others, their mind processes this information to identify how that story is relevant to what they're trying to accomplish. The less relevant, the more mental energy they need to expend to figure out why a more in-depth sales conversation would make sense, which reduces the probability that they will convert.

The Solution: If your company has impressive customers that everyone would recognize, it's tempting to use these stories when talking with prospects on a cold call to give yourself credibility. Resist the temptation until you think for a second.

If your customers include Google, Facebook, and Amazon, it's tempting to put the following phrase on autopilot:

Customers like Google, Facebook, and Amazon trust us to...

OK, if you're talking with a prospect at IBM, then that can work. But what if you're talking to H&C Homebuilders out of northeast Oklahoma? That's right...they don't care.

Customer stories must be relevant in order to build rapport. Telling a small home builder that you work with Google doesn't sound impressive to them, and it is liable to make them think that you only work with big companies, so there's not a compelling reason to continue the conversation.

Organizations must provide their cold callers with an index of customer stories relevant to each market segment that are either memorized or instantly accessible when on a call, such as what's outlined in figure 18.1.

Market Segment	Customer	Pain	Solution	Results
B2B SaasTek	Acme Co.	Can't justify spending in terms of leads, reach, and partnering	Subscribed to SaasTek analysis tool for one year	Reduced their trade show budget by 23% with 33% more revenue impact
Manufacturing	Beta Corp.	Struggled to find the best shows to exhibit at	Subscribed to SaasTek analysis tool for one year	Found 3 shows that produced a 500%+ ROI

Figure 18.1: Example stories by market segment.

Additionally, stories must be relevant at the persona level, so having stories about how you've helped specific people like the individual you're calling is key, as shown in figure 18.2.

Persona	Customer	Pain	Solution	Results
VP Marketing	Acme Co.	Can't justify spending in terms of leads, reach, and partnering	Subscribed to SaasTek analysis tool for one year	Reduced their trade show budget by 23% with 33% more revenue impact
Business Owner	Beta Corp.	Struggled to find the best shows to exhibit at	Subscribed to SaasTek analysis tool for one year	Found 3 shows that produced a 500%+ ROI

Figure 18.2: Stories by persona.

Examples of telling these stories in various scenarios include the following:

Uncovering Pain: Some other marketing leaders I've spoken with often tell me that they're struggling with (pain you solve) and are concerned about (pain you solve). Do either of these issues sound familiar?

Managing Resistance: Can I share how we've worked with other marketing leaders to overcome this exact same concern?

Uncovering Financial Resources: Most companies your size spend $20k–50k per year with us. Is that out of the ballpark?

Be careful not to overuse customer stories. If every sentence out of your mouth is a story, that will damage rapport.

Take Action:

- Build out a customer story to be used with each persona (figure 18.1) and each market segment (figure 18.2).

19

YOU DON'T ASK
FOR THE MEETING

Symptoms:

- You don't schedule as many meetings as other callers on your team.
- Quality conversations during cold calls do not convert to meetings.
- Prospects tell you to follow up with them in the future or to send information.

The Context: Cold call quotas are based on meetings scheduled (or meetings held). Quotas can't be attained if meetings aren't scheduled.

Academically understanding what to do on a cold call is great. Doing parts of what we discuss in these pages gets you on your way to success. But until you consistently schedule meetings from cold calls, you have yet to do your job.

Cold callers can only control two things:

Quantity of Activity: How many dials are made.

Quality of Activity: Who is called and what is said during the call.

The Solution: Ask for the meeting!

Once you find some pain, ask for the meeting! If the prospect pushes back, use the techniques in this book to manage Resistance (questions and active listening), and then ask for the meeting!

If you find that prospects won't convert when you do ask for the meeting, learn from the fails outlined in this book and *take action* to improve the *quality* of your calls. Remember, the only two things within the control of a cold caller are their quantity and quality of activity.

Take Action:

- Ensure that you ask for the meeting each time you have a conversation with a prospect who is your target persona in your target market. If they fail to convert, diagnose possible quality issues with your calls using guidance from this book and take action.

20

YOU DON'T DISQUALIFY BAD LEADS

Symptoms:

- Meetings you set up don't convert through the pipeline.
- Prospects don't show up for the next meeting.

The Context:

A *bad lead* does not fit within your target market, and/or the individual is not a target persona. Even if one or two close from time to time, it will still be a net time waster for the sales team if these leads are consistently converted into opportunities.

Reasons why cold callers fail to disqualify bad leads include:

Desperation: The cold caller is making every attempt to hit his or her quota, including working bad leads.

Expediency: The lead is not vetted against the target market and target personas.

Failure to Identify Bad Lead: The caller doesn't know how to tell if the lead is good or bad.

The Solution: Use the target market matrix from chapter 1 (shown here as figure 20.1) to determine if the lead fits into the target market. If not, they are a bad lead.

Attribute	Rank	Ideal	Good	Rejected
Industry	1	Software	Others	Healthcare
Company Size	2	50–500	10–50, 500–1000	<10, or >1000
Current Solution	3	AlphaCorp	Others	CharlieCo.
Geography	4	US	UK, AUS	Others

Figure 20.1: The target market matrix.

Then, ensure that the lead fits the target personas, as discussed in chapter 2.

Take Action:

- Next time you come across a bad lead that does not fit your target market and target personas, disqualify them and move on.

21

YOU TALK TOO MUCH

Symptoms:

- Lots of activity, little results.
- Calls not converting to meetings.
- Message not resonating.
- Meetings don't hold.
- Call analytics software shows >50% talk time by the caller.

The Context: The whole point of a cold call is to learn if the prospect has (or likely has) pain that can be solved by the caller's company, and if they're willing to take a meeting with a salesperson to explore that possibility. This learning cannot happen when the caller is doing most of the talking.

The Solution: Through the intro, P.L.A.N., and elevator pitch, the cold caller will do most of the talking. The prospect wasn't expecting a call, and they need to figure out why they're on the phone with a stranger. Throughout this section of the cold call framework, the key is to be concise.

After the elevator pitch (and throughout the rest of the sales process!), it's time to shift the majority of the talk time back to the prospect. Figure 21.1 outlines ranges of talk time.

Talk Time	< 50%	50%–65%	65%–75%	75%–85%	>85%
Result	Bad	OK	Ideal	Good	Awkward

Figure 21.1: The percent of time the **prospect** should talk after the elevator pitch.

The value of a salesperson is not measured by the information that they present, but by the information that they receive. People new to cold calling often struggle to find the balance between gathering of information *and* getting a prospect to take a meeting. The key is to understand that:

The best way to demonstrate expertise with prospects is through the quality of your questions.

Asking questions that force a prospect to think critically about their current situation allows them to either realize that they have a problem worth exploring further, or confirm that they don't have such problems. These questions result in the prospect talking a lot about their current state and keeping the cold caller's talk time down.

Remember, however, in order to maintain rapport with the prospect during the call, permission to ask questions has already been granted (chapter 12).

Take Action:

- Record your calls and review your talk time. Either estimate talk time or use call recording software for an accurate measurement. A cold caller's talk time should be between 25% and 35%.

22

YOU DON'T LISTEN

Symptoms:

- You interrupt your prospect.
- You talk more than 35% of the time during a cold call.
- You struggle to capture quality notes during and after the call.
- While the prospect is talking, you find yourself thinking about the next question to ask instead of absorbing what they're saying.

The Context: Prospects constantly provide clues that help you to uncover pain and either convert them to a meeting or disqualify them. The key is that you have to listen to them.

The biggest culprit of cold callers not listening is simple:

They are busy thinking about what to say next.

The Solution: Instead of thinking of questions to ask, the best cold callers leverage *active listening* techniques. People often think that active listening means "paying close attention." That's just the tip of the iceberg.

Active listening is one of the most powerful tools available to a cold caller. It's an interactive and reflective process in which the cold caller continuously focuses on what the prospect is saying with an open mind. This focus means that the cold caller is non-assumptive, non-prejudicial, and non-persuasive throughout the conversation. The cold caller then uses structured responses to fully understand the meaning of the communication.

Effective use of active listening will keep prospects talking while maintaining rapport. Toggling between asking closed-ended pain questions and employing the techniques outlined in this section allows the cold caller to discover large amounts of information about the prospect's business while making their interaction seem more like a conversation and less like an interrogation.

Here are a series of examples of active listening techniques:

Open-ended questions: Questions that refer back to something the prospect said and cannot be answered with a simple yes or no.

> ***Prospect****: We need to find a more effective way to leverage customer data.*

> ***Cold Caller****: How are you leveraging your customer data today?*

Encouragement: Encourages the buyer to go into more detail.

> ***Cold Caller****: I see.* or *Go on.*

Restatement: Repeating the main thought or core of the communication using the buyer's own words.

> ***Cold Caller****: If I understand you correctly . . . or What I hear you saying is . . . or simply restating the last one to four words that the prospect used, causing them to elaborate.*

Silence: Appropriately timed and brief. Usually, this technique is best used after a critical problem has been expressed, such as a cost or a negative emotion.

Paraphrasing: Recapping the core content of the buyer's message in your own words.

> **Prospect**: *If we don't figure out why our customers are buying, we're going to lose market share quickly.*

> **Cold Caller**: *It sounds like understanding buyer behavior is a key to your competitive positioning.*

Reflection: A response that focuses on the feeling, rather than the content, of the communication.

> **Prospect**: *I am managing too many vendors and too much data with too little time.*

> **Cold Caller**: *It sounds like you are frustrated and maybe overwhelmed right now. Is that right?*

Clarifying: Signals the seller's need to more fully understand the buyer's communication.

> **Cold Caller**: *Let me get this straight . . .* or *Can you help me understand . . .*

Empathizing: Verbally acknowledging the buyer's current problem.

> **Cold Caller**: *I can imagine that it's not easy to manage all that while still performing your other functions.*

Each technique keeps the prospect talking. It is not uncommon to have a conversation with a prospect in which the cold caller does roughly 20% of the talking and the prospect walks away thanking them for the great conversation.

Take Action:

- Practice using each of the active listening skills outlined in this chapter. To get comfortable before using these techniques with prospects, try them out with coworkers, friends, and family.

23

YOU SOUND LIKE AN '80S HIGH SCHOOLER

Symptoms:

- Your sentences are littered with filler words.
- Prospects don't seem to open up to you about their pain.
- Calls end abruptly.
- Internally, your coworkers don't take you as seriously as you'd like.

The Context: Juvenile language damages rapport. Getting excited when a prospect is in pain will damage rapport.

> **Cold Caller**: *And what CRM do you use today?*
>
> **Prospect**: *We use Salesforce.*
>
> **Cold Caller**: *Perfect! That's awesome. And how many salespeople are on your team?*
>
> **Prospect**: *There are 30 reps and 4 managers.*
>
> **Cold Caller**: *Excellent! And you're all in Dallas?*
>
> **Prospect**: *Yes.*

Cold Caller: Awesome! That's fabulous!

Beyond the example above, the worst time to use words like *great, awesome, and excellent* is after finding pain.

Cold Caller: Other marketing leaders I'm talking with say that they're struggling to convert leads from trade shows and they're anxious where they should repurpose their marketing dollars. These issues aren't on your radar, are they?

Prospect: Are they? They are both keeping me up at night.

Cold Caller: Awesome! Well, would you like to schedule 30 minutes...

Sadly, we hear this type of thing all the time. Yes, the cold caller is excited because they know they just found pain worthy of scheduling a meeting. However, what does it do to rapport if someone just opened up about their pain, and in return they hear *"awesome?"* Not good. Can you imagine the following exchange with your doctor?

Doctor: When I bend your knee this way, how does that feel?

Patient: Ouch! That hurts so bad.

Doctor: Awesome! When can you block off half-a-day for surgery later this month?

The Solution: If it's not good in the doctor's office, it's not good on a cold call.

Like a doctor, the cold caller's job is to be diagnostic. Identify if the prospect has pain that can be solved with the caller's product or service. If there is an opportunity, the caller can schedule a meeting for their salesperson. If there's not an opportunity, that's a good outcome as well, as the caller can move on to the next prospect and not waste the salesperson's time.

Think about how your doctor acts while being diagnostic. Serious and direct, yet empathetic. That's the ideal posture for a cold caller as well.

Take Action:

- Listen for words like *great, awesome, excellent,* and others in your calls and eliminate them to raise your professionalism and mitigate the risk that this type of language damages rapport.
- Next time you go to the doctor, observe their communication style as they diagnose your problem and either prescribe treatment or disqualify the fact that treatment is needed.

24

YOU REFUSE TO CONSIDER SCRIPTS

Symptoms:

- You constantly find yourself trying to figure out what to say next.
- Looking back on conversations, you frequently see better ways to have handled certain situations.
- You get stumped by prospects.
- You lose your composure during calls.

The Context: We have the following conversation all the time with people who are new to cold calling:

Caller: *I really don't want to sound scripted.*

Cory: *What's your favorite movie?*

Caller: *(names a movie)*

Cory: *Is there a memorable quote from that movie that you think was really delivered well?*

*Caller **(excited to share)***: *Yes! I really liked it when (character) said (line).*

Cory: *Great delivery?*

Caller: *Oh yeah.*

Cory: *And engaging?*

Caller: *Yup.*

Cory: *Any chance that the line from the movie was scripted? You know, maybe in a movie script?*

The Solution: Scripts aren't bad. Poorly delivered scripts are bad. Actors practice their lines, just as folks making cold calls should practice how they deliver over the phone to prospects. In fact, acting skills can go a long way when trying to motivate someone on the other end of the line to take a new meeting. Dramatic pauses, sighs, and changes in tone are all ways to help prospects live the emotional pain they are sharing that will compel them to want to take a meeting.

Good places to start with scripts in a cold calling context include the following:

Call Intro, P.L.A.N., and Elevator Pitch: Have something tight so you don't fumble or talk too much as you work to create the first impression with the prospect.

Customer Stories: Know the specifics around what challenges a customer faced before they worked with your company, the solution you provided, and what results they saw.

Select **Responses to Resistance (Objections)**: As we discuss in chapter 16, the best response to an objection is a question or active listening (chapter 22). In some cases, it's important to have these prepackaged, especially if they are make-or-break objections.

Figure 24.1 breaks down the pros and cons to consider across the various steps of the call framework introduced in chapter 13.

Step	Pros	Cons
Intro	Confident opener and sales person can use the same template regardless of prospect.	N/A
P.L.A.N.	Confidence that call will start on the right path.	N/A
Elevator Pitch	Caller's best chance to earn more time to ask questions and convert the call to a sales opportunity...if the script is relevant to the person being called.	Won't be well-received unless the script is relevant to the person on the other end.
Velocity P.L.A.N.	Create velocity into the next meeting.	Will come off poorly if it sounds out of context, so the actual words need to be adjusted on the fly.
Rest of Call	Use hard-hitting questions and statements that are proven to work.	It's hard to remember which questions and statements to use, and when.

Figure 24.1: Pros and cons of scripts.

Having a fully scripted cold call from end to end is a bad idea. Too much can happen over the course of an entire call for someone to stay on script. However, having scripted snippets that can be used when needed will help a caller to be more confident, effective, and efficient than they would be in a world where each conversation is built from scratch.

We typically find that the more effort someone puts into learning their scripts, the less they need them.

Take Action:

- Identify 1–3 high-risk situations that you expect to face during a cold call and develop scripted messaging to use in these cases.
- Add more scripted snippets over time as you find opportunities to tighten your messaging or improve your confidence.

25

YOU SOUND LIKE A CALLING ROBOT

Symptoms:

- You feel uncomfortable having a peer-to-peer conversation with prospects.
- You believe that you must know the prospect's business in depth to go off-script.
- You stall and struggle with what to say when the prospect says something unexpected.

The Context: In chapter 4, you took a short quiz to identify your business acumen as it relates to prospects. Business acumen is important. You should develop it over time. However, the quest to master business acumen has a flaw:

Your prospects have been working in their business for years. Maybe decades. Any level of effort on your part to understand the prospect's business will still fall short of understanding it as well as they do.

The Solution: Develop the confidence and ability to have a peer-to-peer conversation with any prospect, regardless of their age, title, or company size. Examine the following conversation where a cold caller who knows practically nothing about accounting is talking with a prospect who is an accountant.

> *Prospect*: *See, the problem today is that we have to compile the financial statements from three different data sources, and of course the column headings of the input tables aren't the same, so we have to arm-wrestle the data in a spreadsheet.*

> *Cold Caller*: *That sounds exhausting.*

> *Prospect*: *It really is. Then, when the CFO asks for insight into a specific figure, we usually have to go through the whole process again.*

> *Cold Caller*: *Does the CFO often ask for such insight?*

> *Prospect*: *Yeah, at least once a month.*

> *Cold Caller*: *It sounds like the current system might not be sustainable as you grow.*

> *Prospect*: *I don't think so. I didn't even get into what happens during the end-of-year close.*

> *Cold Caller*: *I'm no accounting expert, but what you're describing sounds like something we've solved for several companies before. Would you like to set up a half-hour call with one of my colleagues to learn more?*

In the exchange above, what business acumen did the cold caller leverage? That's right, absolutely none. They sure did use conversational acumen, however. Active listening (chapter 22). Then a question. Followed by more active listening. And finally a question. Having strong conversational acumen allows someone to navigate any conversation, no matter how technical, by relying mostly on active listening and questioning skills.

Take Action:

- Engage in a conversation with a friend or colleague who is a subject matter expert in a field you know nothing about. Leverage your ability to ask questions and use active listening to manage the conversation.

26

YOU CAN'T GET PAST THE GATEKEEPER

Symptoms:

- You leave messages with gatekeepers that are never returned.
- You have the expected number of conversations (per your prospecting math, chapter 5), but with the wrong people, so conversion rates are lower than expected.
- You can't schedule a meeting if you can't get past the gatekeeper.

The Context: A gatekeeper is anyone who keeps a cold caller from talking with the person they are trying to reach. This person might be a receptionist, an executive assistant, or a junior employee (such as an analyst). Many cold callers believe the following:

Gatekeepers exist to keep salespeople out.

While this statement *can* be true, we view these folks a little differently:

Gatekeepers exist to keep the wrong people out and also to make sure that the right people get in.

This definition breeds the logical question, "well, who are the right people?" If you have called through gatekeepers before, you've heard the following questions:

- "Who is this?"
- "Who are you with?"
- "What's this about?"
- "Are they expecting you?"

The Solution: Simply answering these questions puts the gatekeeper in control of the conversation and greatly increases the chance that access will be blocked. Here's an example of what this approach looks like:

Cold Caller: *May I please speak with Kristen?*

Gatekeeper: *Who is this?*

Cold Caller: *Coldy McCaller*

Gatekeeper: *Who are you with?*

Cold Caller: *SaasTek. An online technology company.*

Gatekeeper: *What's this about?*

Cold Caller: *I'm following up on an email I sent yesterday about how we might be able to work together.*

Gatekeeper: *Is she expecting your call?*

Cold Caller: *I mentioned in the email that I was going to call her.*

What do you think happens next? That's right, the gatekeeper takes a message, and the caller hangs up. Maybe the gatekeeper asks for the caller to "send some information."

Let's look at an alternative approach where the caller takes and maintains control of the situation but does not cross the line of lying to the gatekeeper, which is never OK.

Always remember that the person asking the questions controls the conversation, so get off your heels.

Cold Caller: Hi it's <name>. For Kristen. Is she around?

Gatekeeper: Who is this?

Cold Caller: It's <name>, who's this?

Gatekeeper: This is John.

Cold Caller: (hurried) Hey John, I'm just trying to reach her before my next call. Is she available?

Gatekeeper: Umm . . . who are you with?

Cold Caller: Who am I with? It's just me here right now. Sounds like she's still busy. Is that right?

Gatekeeper: (flustered) Is she expecting your call?

Cold Caller: I'm not sure. You know I have a bit of a tight schedule, and I don't want to waste your time either—should I just go to voicemail?

Does this work every time? No. But why sit back and wait for the gate-keeper to ask the questions that box you in? The idea here is not a script; the idea is to take control of the conversation and get accustomed to asking questions. The tone is not antagonistic but has just an air of full expectation that the caller should be able to speak to Kristen.

Interrupt the pattern. Whatever a typical salesperson is doing, you should be doing differently.

Take Action:

- Write your answers to the following questions: Who is this? Who are you with? What's this about? Are they expecting you? Role play until your responses roll off your tongue without triggering any cold sweats or anxiety. Then practice it on real-life calls.

27

PROSPECTS NO-SHOW YOUR NEXT MEETING

Symptoms:

- Prospects agree to meet, but don't accept the calendar invite you send.
- Prospects accept the calendar invite, but they are no-shows anyways.

The Context: Many cold callers get paid not based on the number of meetings *scheduled*, but rather the number of meetings *held*, meaning that the prospects actually show up.

Imagine the following scenario where Michael is a senior executive and Scottie is a manager at a prospect company:

Scottie: Can you come to this meeting at 10:00 in conference room 23?

Michael: I'm slammed. What's the meeting about?

Scottie: Some folks are doing a demo of their accounting software.

Do you think Michael is going to show up? Not very compelling, right? What about this scenario:

> **Scottie**: *Can you come to this meeting at 10:00 in conference room 23?*
>
> **Michael**: *I'm slammed. What's the meeting about?*
>
> **Scottie**: *Some folks who said they can fix that sales tax issue you've been complaining about forever. They are also going to also show how to eliminate our FCPA liability compliance that our lawyers keep price-gouging us on.*

What about now? Michael has context around real pain. If this pain resonates, then he'll probably show up.

If a prospect no-shows for a meeting, the best question to ask yourself is:

> *When this person's boss saw the meeting on their calendar and asked what it was, how did they respond?*

Was the meeting important? Urgent? A low priority? Or worse, did they just say to send them an invite to get off the phone during the cold call?

If the prospect can't clearly articulate why they will show up for the next meeting, why would they? And even if they can, where does showing up fit on their long list of priorities?

The Solution: An exercise to test if prospects have a compelling reason to show up is to fill out figure 27.1 with info about three upcoming meetings you've booked. Here we want to highlight what pain we have uncovered. If the prospect doesn't have a serious pain point to solve, either they will deprioritize the meeting and not show up, or they don't have a compelling reason to buy, so they will waste the salesperson's time. Neither scenario is good.

Prospect Name	Why Would They Show Up? What Pain Do They Have?
Karen	Missing lead quota
John	Large # of leads are rejected
Pat	Excessive rework leads to missed deadlines

Figure 27.1: Why would your prospects show up?

Take Action:

- Create your own version of figure 27.1 for upcoming prospect meetings.

28

YOUR CALLS DON'T MATCH YOUR ROLE PLAYS

Symptoms:

- You're frequently caught off guard.
- You are always thinking about what to say next.
- You feel like a *lack of experience* is why you're lagging on performance compared to other teammates.

The Context:

By failing to prepare, you are preparing to fail.

—Ben Franklin

An academic understanding of what to do on a cold call is not going to prepare someone for when a prospect says _____. Role plays are required. If you're not role playing, that's a problem. If you still find that you frequently end up in uncharted territory on the phone with prospects, it means that your calls don't match your role plays.

Most cold callers only have a handful of conversations per day, and they happen at unpredictable and sporadic times. The good news is that a limited number of scenarios will happen during these calls, and these can be practiced. Hence, mistakes are made and learned from in a practice setting, thereby improving performance when it's game time.

The Solution: Any common scenario that comes up in a cold call should be documented and callers should frequently role play each. Schedule role plays with teammates and also create a *culture of role play*.

For structured role plays, ensure that the following are defined:

Characters: One person is the prospect, and one is the caller. The prospect's persona, market segment, and other relevant information must be defined. The depth of the prospect's character should match what the caller would encounter in the real world, which might not be much information.

Scenario: Start the role play at either the top of the call or at a specific point, such as when the prospect has offered up Resistance.

Desired Outcome: The scope of the role play could vary from "manage this Resistance" to "complete the call."

In a highly structured role play with a manager and his or her team, the structure might look like the following:

Manager: We're going to run some role plays. First, Phil will be the salesperson and Toni will be the prospect. Toni is the VP of marketing at a 500-person insurance company who has had no prior interaction with us. Phil's goal is to schedule a meeting between Toni and Phil's salesperson.

At this point, Phil and Toni get into character and role play.

Another scenario that we highly recommend that teams adopt is the ad hoc role play. Everyone on your team (including management) should be empowered to walk up to cold callers in the hallways, in the lunchroom, or via phone (for remote teams) and say things like, "We are going to build our own solution in-house." Reacting to these statements out of the blue will lessen the surprise when they are heard on the phone.

Here we find Phil and Toni in the lunchroom (which can be replaced by a chat message for remote teams):

Toni: *Hey Phil, do you have a minute?*

Phil: *Sure. What's up?*

Toni: *I'm your prospect. A VP of marketing at a 200-person financial advisory firm. You just delivered your elevator pitch. Ready?*

Phil: *Go.*

Toni: *Phil, I don't think we need to chat. We're happy with our current solution.*

Toni gave Phil some context, but not too much. Folks with mastery can be dropped into a scenario like this one and shine. Those who do not have mastery will struggle. The key is to identify if you or your team struggles in specific scenarios, and then work on them!

The bottom line is that if someone can't perform well in a role play with coworkers, they're going to struggle to manage the same situation with a cold senior executive on the other end of the line. Getting caught off guard with a scenario that has never been practiced or hasn't been revisited for weeks is negligent.

Take Action:

- Schedule role plays with peers or your manager.
- Create opportunities for ad hoc role plays to make sure that you can manage scenarios on the fly, as they would appear in the real world.

29

YOU DON'T ASK FOR REFERRALS

Symptoms:

- You don't hit your goals and don't ask prospects for referrals.
- It's challenging to get meetings with multiple stakeholders within one company.

The Context: Cold conversations are hard. One way to guarantee that each of your conversations remains cold and challenging is to avoid asking for referrals. We often ask people if they ask for referrals and hear, "sure, sometimes," but when we dig in deeper, we realize that *sometimes* doesn't mean the same thing for everyone.

Referrals are often the lowest-effort prospects a cold caller will encounter, but they have to ask to get them.

The Solution: To keep yourself honest and figure out if you actually ask for referrals, fill out figure 29.1 with the actual number of times you have asked for a referral and the number of times one was received. Internal referrals are to other people inside of a prospect's organization, while external referrals are to folks at other companies.

Type of Referral	# of Referral Asks	Referrals Received
Internal	7	3
External	3	1

Figure 29.1: The four-week referral tracker.

How do your numbers look? Would you want to show your results to your head of sales or CEO? If not, that's fine; it's just between you and this book, at least for now. Let's work on how to improve your performance by asking for referrals.

Navigating Referrals
Referrals come in many flavors. You can earn referrals to different people, departments, companies, divisions of companies, conferences, or groups. Sometimes a prospect will offer up a referral by saying something like, "You know, you really should reach out to Cletus in our Topeka office," but often it's not that easy, and you have to ask.

Let's look at possible language to use in several referral scenarios below.

Wrong Person at Right Company (Internal Referral):
Based on what you know about us so far, do you have an idea who I should talk to in your organization?

Right Person at Right Company (Internal Referral):
Typically our customers will want to include (others who should be included) at some point. Do you think it makes sense to do so now?

Right Person at Right Company (External Referral):
I'm glad we're going to be able to connect again next week. It might be premature to ask, but do you know anyone else in your network that might be interested in a conversation around (pain you're solving)?

Right Person at Wrong Company:
It sounds like you're all set. Based on what you've heard about us, is there anyone else in your network that you think I should speak with?

Much more important than the language is the fact that you're asking. Figure out what language works for you and ask away. It's nearly impossible to get quality referrals without initiating the conversation.

Take Action:

- Calculate your current rate of referrals in figure 29.1, and identify if there is a plan to improve.

SECTION 3: INBOUND LEADS

30

YOU THINK INBOUND LEADS ARE EASY

Symptoms:

- Almost all of your inbound lead conversions come from meeting or demo requests, and not from other forms of inbound activity.
- Inbound lead conversion rates are lower than expected.
- You fail to uncover pain when talking with inbound prospects.
- Inbound leads no-show for their scheduled meetings with salespeople.

The Context: Many people don't consider a call to an inbound lead to be a cold call, and that's a huge mistake.

We often ask companies the following question:

When a prospect goes to your website and downloads a white paper, what do we know?

Answers we hear typically include the following:

- "They are interested in our business."
- "They have a problem we can help to solve."
- "They are a hot lead."

In fact, the prospect has simply downloaded a white paper. Nothing more. We can't even infer that they have read it.

The Solution:

If you've had a desk in an open-floor plan, you've inevitably heard the following (use your best monotone expression):

> *(Prospect Name). This is Coldy McCaller. From SaasTek. The reason for my call is that you expressed some interest in our product. And I wanted to set up a 20-minute introductory meeting with my colleague. Is there a time that works in the next few days?*

Maybe (Prospect Name) says yes since a call is a logical follow-up to the asset download. Maybe they don't know off the top of their head what Coldy is talking about. Either way, this approach does nothing to create velocity toward another meeting.

Figure 30.1 demonstrates how to index all downloadable assets against likely pain for inbound leads.

Asset Downloaded	Persona	Likely Pain
Dashboards white paper	CMO	Struggle to make data-driven decisions around marketing spend
		Concerned about competitive pressures
	Marketing Manager	Frustrated there is no single source of truth for marketing analytics
Security white paper	IT	Anxious about moving key data to the cloud

Figure 30.1: Index of activities vs. call openers.

Given figure 30.1, the previous opening script can now be transformed into the following:

> **Cold Caller**: *(Prospect Name). This is Coldy from SaasTek. That name probably doesn't ring a bell?*

Prospect: Yes, I know AlphaCorp. I was on your site recently.

Cold Caller: Exactly, and that's why I'm giving you a ring today. In 30 seconds I can tell you specifically why I called, and then you can decide if we keep talking. Is that fair?

Prospect: Sure.

Cold Caller: I saw that you downloaded our dashboard's white paper. Typically when I see a CMO download this asset, it's because they're struggling to make data-driven decisions around marketing spend or they're concerned about competitive pressures. Do either of these points seem relevant?

Now, the cold caller is a business person having a business conversation. They are no longer begging a CMO to take another meeting because of some action they may or may not remember taking. Instead, the caller is using the S.C.A.N. framework from chapter 9 to identify pain that would create a compelling reason for the prospect to take a meeting with the caller's salesperson.

Take Action:

- Ensure that you uncover at least one pain point before scheduling a meeting for your salesperson with inbound leads.

31

YOU TREAT ALL INBOUND LEADS THE SAME

Symptoms:

- Almost all of your inbound lead conversions come from meeting or demo requests, and not from other forms of inbound activity.
- Inbound lead conversion rates are lower than expected.
- You fail to uncover pain when talking with inbound prospects.
- Inbound leads no-show for their scheduled meetings with salespeople.

The Context: Think about the different between the following types of leads:

1. **Meeting Request**: Someone explicitly said they want to meet or see a demo of your product.
2. **Free Trial Sign-up**: A prospect wanted to put their hands on your product to see what it might be able to do for them.
3. **Online Asset Download**: A headline and/or summary caught their eye and they wanted to take a closer look.
4. **Intent Data**: The prospect did something in the background, such as looked at your website, but never converted. A third-party data provider gave you a heads-up that something happened.

People in the first group obviously want to have a meeting, so we wouldn't consider these cold calls. However, the others may or may not be there yet, and as a result, they shouldn't be treated as *hot leads* without further inspection.

The Solution: First, determine the different sources of inbound leads and their associated conversion rates. Then augment this information with a hypothesis on how to improve the conversion rate, as shown in figure 31.1.

Source	Conversion Rate	How to Improve Conversion
Request for Meeting	85%	Don't give up if rapid conversion doesn't happen.
Free Trial Sign-up	25%	Tie messaging to what they have done in the trial.
Online Asset Download	12%	Ensure that messaging is relevant to why someone like them would care about the asset they downloaded.
Intent Data	7%	Use our normal calling framework instead of trying to hard-close a meeting.

Figure 31.1: Inbound lead sources and conversion rates.

If conversion rates are lower than expected, the *How to Improve* column should include discovery techniques, including improving the quality of pain-based discovery (using S.C.A.N. questions, chapter 9). An example for using this framework with inbound leads was presented in the previous chapter.

Take Action:

- Identify a way to improve inbound lead conversion rates for each line item covered in figure 31.1 for your workflow. If you don't manage inbound leads, skip this activity.

32

YOU TRY TO HARD-CLOSE LEADS DUE TO INTENT

Symptoms:

- Inbound leads with strong intent are not converting to meetings.
- Meetings scheduled with prospects who have strong intent scores are not holding.
- You are not uncovering pain when speaking with leads that have intent.

The Context: *Intent data* refers to insights that a prospect is actively researching the type of product or service that you sell. Intent data is often sold to several competitors, so the prospect is already being (or soon will be) bombarded with calls and emails from your competitors. As a result, you must stand out when calling leads that surfaced due to intent data.

A mistake that we often see is as follows:

> **Cold Caller**: *Hi, this is Coldy with SaasTek. I got word from our partner LeadCo that you're in the market for (THE TYPE OF SOFTWARE WE SELL). Is that right?*
>
> **Prospect**: *Well, I might be.*

Cold Caller: I'm calling to set up a thirty-minute call with my product specialist to answer some of your questions and better understand your needs. Do you have time later this week for a call? Maybe on Thursday?

Prospect: Sure. Thursday at 3:00 p.m. works.

If we're simply looking at outcomes, it looks like the caller is doing a great job. They got the prospect to agree to a meeting, and they did it fast. There is no clear reason why this prospect would take a meeting, but the caller isn't worried about that yet. First, they need to make sure that they don't get in trouble for handing the salesperson a bad lead, so next they need to *qualify* the prospect, even though they have already made an offer of a meeting, which has been accepted.

Caller: Great. Before I get that on the books, can I ask three quick questions?

Prospect: Sure.

Caller: How many people at your company would use our software?

Prospect: Well, I'm not sure. Maybe 5. Maybe 20. Heck, it could be upward of 100. I'm not sure.

Caller: And I have that your headquarters is located in Georgia. Is that correct?

Prospect: Well, I'm in Georgia. Last year a company out of Ukraine bought us in a joint venture with a Dutch...maybe it was a Danish company.

Caller: So your U.S. headquarters is in Georgia?

Prospect: Well, this is our biggest office, but most of our executives are in New York.

Caller: OK. Thanks for that. And as far as a timeline for when you want to make a purchase. What are you thinking? The next three months?

Prospect: Well, maybe. I don't even know what your company has to offer yet. So that's hard to say. Maybe three months. Maybe a year. Heck, maybe never, you know?

Hopefully this exchange doesn't sound familiar, but if it does, let's fix it.

Third-party websites will harvest leads from prospects and sell the data to many vendors, leaving it to them to follow up and make contact. The workflow can be as follows:

1. Prospect goes to a third-party site, such as an analyst firm that writes reviews about different types of products or services.
2. Prospect provides their contact information in exchange for some type of information.
3. The third-party site provides the contact information to your company. Previously, your company had either subscribed to this data or agreed to pay on a per-lead basis.
4. These leads pop up in your queue to call.

Check with your marketing team to confirm if this is the case for your organization or not, but with step 3 above, most intent companies do not only sell you lead data, but they'll sell the exact same lead to several of your competitors as well. There's no problem with this activity on the surface, since it's common practice; your marketing team was likely aware of it, and the prospect was in the act of researching alternatives.

The Solution: Even for calls where there's clear intent, leverage the framework built out in chapter 13. The minute folks try to take shortcuts on cold calls they start hitting walls and spend more time backing up than moving forward, letting valuable opportunities slip through the cracks along the way.

Also, it's key to understand how many other companies have access to your intent data. Many data providers will sell the same leads to multiple companies, so if your call uses the same high-pressure messaging as your competition, it's going to be tough to set yourself apart, and it will be a turnoff to the prospect.

Take Action:

- Ensure that you are uncovering pain even if the prospect has shown intent.

33

YOUR EVENT FOLLOW-UP ISN'T COMPELLING

Symptoms:

- Leads are not converting to meetings after events at the expected rate.
- Post-event language isn't relevant to the prospect.

The Context: Think about the following example:

Cold Caller: Hi, Marty, this is Coldy with SaasTek. You met some of my colleagues at TradeshowWorld last week in Las Vegas?

Prospect: Oh yeah. How's it going?

Cold Caller: Good. How are you?

Prospect: Oh, can't complain. Long week with the show last week.

Cold Caller: I bet. The reason I'm actually reaching out today is that, like I said, you met some of my colleagues, and what I'd love to do is to set up a 30-minute exploratory conversation for you to learn a little bit more about what we do. Do you have time later this week to set that up?

This guy (Marty) literally came to your tradeshow booth a week ago to learn a little about what you do. Now, he's back at his office catching up on work after having been out for a week. What is his appetite to spend more time exploring what you do?

The Solution: Companies with strong event playbooks have a process to ensure that the follow-up team gets as much insight into what was discussed during the event. Imagine the following conversation:

> *Cold Caller: Hi, Marty, this is Coldy with SaasTek. You met some of my colleagues at TradeshowWorld last week in Las Vegas?*

> *Prospect: Oh yeah. How's it going?*

> *Cold Caller: Good. How are you?*

> *Prospect: Oh, can't complain. Long week with the show last week.*

> *Cold Caller: My notes here show that you chatted with Karen a bit and expressed some concern that your pay-per-click leads were converting to initial conversations, but not to closed business. Does that sound right?*

> *Prospect: Don't remind me! That's what I need to work on this week.*

> *Cold Caller: Well, with that being the case, would it make sense to reconnect with Karen to explore how we have helped other folks like yourself diagnose and fix problems like these?*

A subtle change between how these conversations are positioned makes a world of difference.

While referring to specific conversations that happened at the event is ideal, if none happened, that's OK. Some events, such as those held online, wouldn't support one-on-one conversations anyways.

Cold Caller: Hi, Marty, this is Pat with SaasTek. You came to our webinar last week?

Prospect: Oh yeah. How's it going?

Cold Caller: Pretty good. I wanted to see if you have 3 minutes to give me some feedback on the webinar.

Think about this question in terms of the S.C.A.L.E. framework (chapter 3):

Status was elevated since they were asked for feedback.

Certainty was created with the 3-minute ask.

Autonomy was not violated in any way, as it would have been if the initial ask was to schedule another meeting with the salesperson (though that can still happen on this call).

Likeness wasn't impacted either way.

Equity was maintained, as the ask for 3 minutes of feedback seems like an equitable exchange for the information provided in the webinar.

The best cold callers not only know that they should build and maintain rapport but also take every opportunity available to measure it against the S.C.A.L.E. drivers as we did here.

Following the feedback, the caller will have an idea of where to focus their pain-based discovery question.

Take Action:

- If you call after in-person or digital events, update your approach with the content from this chapter.

SECTION 4: ACTIVITY

34

YOUR QUANTITY IS TOO LOW

Symptoms:

- The quantity of activity is too low for you to achieve your goals.

The Context: Fierce debates rage around if prospectors should optimize for quantity or quality. Both sides of the debate have reasonable points, with the quality folks saying that without quality, it will be hard to generate results. On the other side of the argument sit the people saying that without quantity, it's impossible to hit goals, even with the highest levels of quality.

The Solution: Our stance on the quantity vs. quality debate is simple: optimize for quantity, given that each activity is above a certain level of quality. Figure 34.1 outlines this concept.

Figure 34.1: Quantity, above a given level of quality.

Using the outcomes of your *prospecting math* exercise (chapter 5), identify what your cold calling quantity should be. Prospecting math identified the average number of dials per day needed to achieve goals.

The key is that this quantity must be sustained over time. Figure 34.2 outlines what happens when quantity goals are missed for a period of time.

Scenario	Day 1	Day 2	Day 3	Day 4	Day 5
Call Goal	80	80	80	80	80
Actual	50	50	90	90	90
Make Up Required	30	60	50	40	30

Figure 34.2: Coming from behind.

In figure 34.2, the cold caller had a goal of 80 dials per day, but only made 50 on days 1 and 2. As a result, they were 60 dials behind going into day 3. Even though the caller outperformed vs. their activity goal on days 3–5, they still ended the week with 30 fewer calls than expected. Due to constraints around how many dials someone can physically make in a day and the hours during which dials are effective, it's hard or impossible to come from behind.

Take Action:

- If you are not certain of the number already, identify the number of dials needed on a daily basis to hit your goals.
- Put an easy-to-update process in place to track actual vs. expected activity.

35

YOUR QUALITY IS TOO LOW

Symptoms:

- You are calling the right people in the right companies, but not scheduling meetings.
- Your manager has brought up concerns about the quality of your conversations and/or handoffs.

The Context: Examples of how low quality is observed in a cold call include the following:

Relevance: If messaging isn't relevant to a prospect, they won't engage.

Credibility: Incredible claims damage rapport, and it might only take one to be pushed past the point of no return.

Call-to-Action: An unclear or irrelevant call-to-action will not receive prospect engagement. Additionally, if the CTA is too big of an ask, it will be ignored.

Figure 35.1 shows that the lower the quality of work, the more is the effort required to achieve goals.

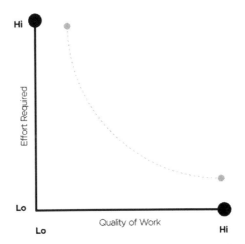

Figure 35.1: Low quality requires high effort to produce results.

The Solution: Identify the minimum level of quality that will consistently convert calls into scheduled meetings.

If you're like most people we've worked with and have a thorough understanding of the *pain finder* (chapter 8), a strong structure for your calls (chapter 13), the ability to tell relevant customer stories (chapter 18), and strong active listening skills (chapter 22), you're probably in good shape. Add in additional learnings from this book as you hit walls during your conversations.

Excessive research and personalization does not equate to a substantially higher probability of converting a call to an opportunity. Consider the following example where a cold caller had a short conversation with a CMO who had just expressed frustration to an internal colleague about their inability to make data-driven decisions around marketing spend prior to receiving the cold call.

> **Cold Caller (mid-call)**: *A lot of CMOs I speak with tell me that they're struggling to make data-driven decisions around marketing spend. I don't suppose you've run into this challenge, have you?*

What is the CMO going to say? That they don't want to talk more because the cold caller didn't read their blog posts? Research their LinkedIn profile? Do some other type of busywork research?

Cold callers who struggle with quality often turn to *more research*, when in fact they should instead focus on sharpening their skills as outlined above and in other chapters in this book. Only when these are mastered should heavy research be considered as the best opportunity to convert conversations to meetings.

Take Action:

- Define what the minimum level of quality is to have an effective cold call in your market.

36

YOU DON'T SEEK FEEDBACK FROM YOUR MANAGER

Symptoms:

- You feel like you're not getting better at you job each month.
- Mistakes are repeated.
- Your manager does not provide constructive criticism of your job performance.
- It feels like your manager underestimates you, but you don't know why.

The Context: Your manager has the ability to make you better via feedback. Some will be offered up proactively, but the best feedback is often explicitly sought by the cold caller.

Here are some of the reasons why your manager might give great feedback:

Experience: If they have done your job before, you can learn from their mistakes.

Perspective: They manage a lot of people who do what you do, so they are able to help you learn from the mistakes of others and replicate the success of those who are doing well.

Insights: Beyond working with your team, managers work with other departments to learn insights into your company and the broader marketplace. Many of these can be leveraged to improve your job and your overall career.

The Solution: Create a cadence with which you will proactively seek feedback from your manager. We recommend doing so weekly so that there is ample opportunity to improve over time.

There are three paths a cold caller can take when receiving feedback:

Ignore It: Nod your head to end the conversation as fast as possible, and then fail to implement any feedback received.

Fight It: Push back that the feedback isn't relevant.

Apply It: Take the feedback and apply it, with the goal of getting better.

The obvious best choice is to apply it. Better yet, apply it and close the loop by reviewing what happened as a result the subsequent time you meet with your manager.

Take Action:

- Next time you meet with your manager, ask for feedback, apply it, and then demonstrate what impact applying the feedback had next time you meet.

37

YOU DON'T SEEK FEEDBACK
FROM SALESPEOPLE

Symptoms:

- You feel like you're not getting better at you job each month.
- Mistakes are repeated.
- Your manager does not provide constructive criticism of your job performance.
- It feels like your manager underestimates you, but you don't know why.
- Salespeople reject your leads without providing helpful feedback on what to do differently next time.

The Context: The best cold callers follow up with the salespeople they schedule meetings for to get feedback on the quality of leads that they pass, as well as the notes that they sent over from their cold call. When cold callers set meetings for salespeople, the salespeople are in a great position to provide feedback on why the meeting set was or wasn't good.

The Solution: Figure 37.1 outlines a passed lead feedback form that can be reviewed verbally, via email, via chat, or in the CRM. On the surface, this exercise creates "more work" for the salesperson, but the benefit is that it provides critical coaching to ensure future passed leads are as good as or better than past leads.

Category	Score	Notes
Market Segment	3	Right in our target market.
Persona	2	Director is OK. Prefer VP.
Pain	2	Need to dig in more, but good start.
Notes	3	Notes were concise & thorough.

Figure 37.1: Passed lead feedback form (for score, 0 = bad, 1 = OK, and 2 = good).

Create your own scorecard in figure 37.2, using categories that are relevant to your business. If your manager or sales enablement team don't currently encourage quick feedback from salespeople on passed leads, talk to them about it as a potential growth opportunity for folks making cold calls.

Category	Score	Notes

Figure 37.2: Passed lead feedback form (for score, 0 = bad, 1 = OK, and 2 = good).

Take Action:

- Get together with salespeople you schedule meetings for and ask for their feedback on your performance. Specifically, ask about your ability to target the right market and the right persona, identify pain, and take good notes.

38

YOU DON'T MANAGE YOUR TIME WELL

Symptoms:

- Failure to achieve activity goals.
- Poor CRM hygiene.
- Sloppy prospect handoffs to your salesperson.
- No time to focus on learning and professional development.
- A constant feeling of being in a rush or behind.

The Context: People with bad time management skills don't get enough activity done and/or they focus their attention on the wrong activities. Poor time management skills can doom a cold caller. Messaging distractions, human interruptions, and snack attacks can take an otherwise productive person and turn them into a low-output cost center for their organization.

The Solution: Let's review three time management techniques that we have seen work well for cold callers: the Eisenhower matrix, the 4 Cs, and pomodoros.

Time Management Strategy: The Eisenhower Matrix

President Eisenhower famously prioritized his work based on its urgency and importance. As a result, the Eisenhower matrix was born, as shown in figure 38.1.

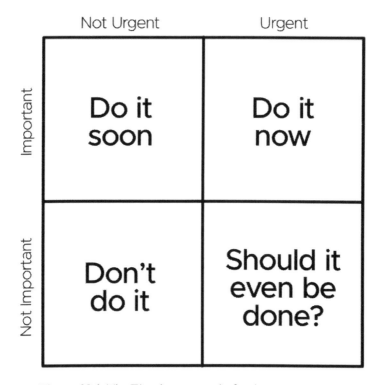

Figure 38.1: The Eisenhower matrix for time management.

Use figure 38.1 to plot all of your weekly tasks that take more than 5 minutes across the 4 quadrants as follows:

Urgent and Important: These tasks must be completed right now. An example is sending a calendar invite for a meeting between a prospect and a salesperson before the available slots get filled. Do this task now.

Not Urgent and Important: These tasks must be completed, but not immediately. Updates to the CRM and developing a prospect list fit into this category.

Urgent and Not Important: Interruptions to your day often fall into this category. Phone calls, chat messages, or colleagues tapping you on the shoulder result in your urgent attention, but the activity is often not important.

Not Urgent and Not Important: Avoid this quadrant at all costs.

Once your tasks are plotted, first figure out which ones you can eliminate from your workflow. Then, identify if there are certain tasks that can be moved from the urgent and important category to the not urgent and important quadrant. As a result, the urgent nature of getting this work done will reduce the interruption to your day.

Time Management Tactics: The Four Cs of Time Management
The four things to keep in mind when managing your time are as follows:

Calendar: Put items on your calendar and hold yourself accountable to doing what's calendared.

Cease: Stop doing things that are not required and don't work toward your goals.

Consign: Delegate tasks to other people or to software that will automate the tasks.

Chunk: Focus on one task at a time instead of constantly switching back and forth.

Applying the four Cs will help make sure that you are more productive, as the human brain is horrible at multitasking and task switching.

Calendar chunking is a term used to describe blocking off specific periods of time to focus on specific tasks.

Advanced Calendar Tactic: Pomodoros

One of our favorite time management techniques is the pomodoro. Used widely by software developers and other knowledge workers who find breaking focus detrimental to productivity, the pomodoro both forces focus and forces breaks, optimizing the person's ability to get things done.

A typical pomodoro cycle is as follows:

> **Work** for 25 minutes
> **Break** for 5 minutes
> **Work** for 25 minutes
> **Break** for 5 minutes
> **Work** for 25 minutes
> **Break** for 5 minutes
> **Work** for 25 minutes
> **Break** for 30 minutes
> **Repeat**

When you're "on-pom," meaning that you're in the *work* phase, close email and chat, and put your phone away. When you're "off-pom," or on a break, put your work away and do whatever you want. If you struggle to focus on a task without being constantly distracted, the pomodoro technique might be a great option to help boost productivity.

To get started, find a highly rated free pomodoro chrome extension to add to your browser.

Take Action:

- Over the course of the next week, plot your time allocation on the Eisenhower matrix.

- Based on what you uncover with your Eisenhower matrix, determine how you can calendar, cease, consign, and chunk different activities.
- Try the pomodoro system and observe what impact it has on your productivity.

39

YOU RESEARCH TOO MUCH

Symptoms:

- You feel like you don't have enough time to make calls because of the amount of research you're doing.
- You are researching before each dial.

The Context: Too much research takes time away from quantity and increases the probability that goals won't be met. To demonstrate what too much research looks like in a cold calling scenario, imagine Coldy McCaller, a sales development rep who needs to schedule 15 meetings a month with prospects. Prior to calling Acme Corp, Coldy does the following:

1. Searches through LinkedIn and finds Terry, the ideal prospect to call at Acme.
2. Does background research on Terry and realizes that Gonzaga basketball is the best icebreaker.
3. Researches her sales playbook and identifies the key pain point that her product can solve for Acme.
4. Does some research on Acme's industry.

5. Reads three news articles that talk about Acme.
6. Calls Terry.
7. No one answers.

The process above is exhausting. At the opposite extreme, Coldy might have just called Terry knowing nothing else other than her company name and title.

The question then arises, *Where is the line in the sand between "not enough research" and "too much"?* It's really easy to read Internet posts that say research and personalization are important and you nod your head along the way, but at some point excessive quality prevents goals from being met.

Additionally, the amount of time spent in research has a direct correlation to the emotional investment of the caller in the lead. It's dangerous for a caller to be emotionally tied to any one prospect since they convince themselves that the lead should be a customer and therefore become less inquisitive.

The Solution: The easiest answer is that knowing the prospect's market segment (chapter 1) and persona (chapter 2) typically provides enough information to ask a couple of pain-based discovery questions and identify if there's a reason to schedule a meeting or not. Going deeper into research can create a richer conversation, but the goal isn't to have a robust dialogue; it's to figure out if there's a compelling reason to schedule a meeting for a salesperson and the prospect.

An overfocus on research results in:

Excessive Time Not Calling: Ideally the cold caller just focuses on having conversations, though they might have to do minimal prep to make sure that the dials are going to the right personas in the right market segments.

Call Reluctance: Humans can spend lots of time talking themselves into why something won't work, or, in this case, why they're not ready to make calls.

Lack of Activity: Every minute a cold caller spends researching is a minute they are not calling.

Too much focus on research results in a lot of busywork that produces no results. It's like folding shirts in a department store. The shirts are folded, but that doesn't generate any revenue.

Take Action:

- Define the minimum amount of research needed for you to have relevant pain-based conversations with your prospects. Hint: it's not much.

40

YOU RESEARCH THE WRONG THINGS

Symptoms:

- Any part of the research done does not directly translate to getting a meeting scheduled with a prospect.
- Research time is spent on superficial items that have nothing to do with uncovering pain.
- You feel like you don't have enough time to make calls because of the amount of research you're doing.
- You are researching before each dial.

The Context: In the ideal world, cold callers don't do research; they simply have conversations, book meetings, and feed insights back to their research teams. However, that's not always the case, so for the purpose of this chapter, assume that the caller does his or her own research.

The Solution: Determine the specific items that must be researched in order to make effective cold calls.

At a basic level, you must determine the prospect's company, the contacts to call within each company, and the contacts' personas. This information provides enough to have a pain-based conversation using the call framework presented in chapter 13. For many callers, this is all the research that needs to be done.

Beyond this basic info, research *triggers* focus on companies *most likely* want to have a conversation with your sales team *now*. Common answers include the following:

Recent M&A Activity: A company that recently acquired another one was acquired itself, or merged with a like-sized organization.

Recent Funding: Raised a large amount of venture capital, private equity, public equity, or debt.

Hiring Activity: They are hiring in general, or hiring for specific roles.

News: Specific news that is relevant to your business.

However, the word *research* could have different meanings here, as triggers like these can be pushed to callers in the form of alerts if you have the right software subscriptions.

If you are focusing research efforts on anything else, ask yourself: How (specifically) does this item directly impact my ability to convert calls into scheduled meetings?

Take Action:

- Determine the minimum number of items that need to be researched in order to make effective cold calls. Note that for some people, this number might be zero, since key facts such as persona, market segment, and triggers are pushed to them via technology.

- Identify specific triggers that indicate that the timing is right for a conversation with a prospect and determine how to surface these with the least amount of effort possible.

41

YOUR RESEARCH IS INEFFICIENT

Symptoms:

- You fail to hit quantity goals, despite heavy research.
- You spend time on research that should be used making calls.
- You don't use dedicated research blocks of time, but rather, you research continuously.

The Context: For every minute that a caller spends researching, that's 1 minute that they aren't talking with prospects.

The Solution: Identify opportunities to improve research efficiency and then execute.

A tried and true method of identifying inefficiency is the time and motion study. This technique allows one to observe the time that it takes to do various tasks and the motions that are required to complete them. A simple version of this concept that a cold caller or their team can conduct is as follows:

1. For a period of one week, keep track of every minute spent doing research.

2. Map out the specific process for doing research from start to finish. Include what happened to identify that it was time to start researching, and then track every step, including clicks between screens or technology products on the path to conducting research.

If the process in step 2 varied at all during the week, take note of these variances and explain why they exist.

After the study is complete, identify areas for improvement, and make a list of where you will make changes. We often find the following opportunities:

Eliminate Steps: If the step does not directly impact the caller's ability to schedule a meeting with a prospect, it should be eliminated.

Focus Energy: Use the *chunk* and *calendar* tactics in the time management chapter (chapter 38) to focus on getting research done at once and then move on to making calls.

Delegate Steps: If another person is able to do the work, explore that option.

Automate Steps: Use technology to replace manual work.

If any of these options are outside your control, work with your manager on making them a reality.

Take Action:

- Identify ways to increase research efficiency, and then put these changes into action.

42

TAKING NOTES IS A DISTRACTION

Symptoms:

- You struggle to take good notes during cold calls.
- You struggle to ask good questions while taking notes.
- Your salespeople complain about the quality of your notes.

The Context: If you've made cold calls before, you would have run into the note-taking paradox:

> *Humans have a tough time listening and writing at the same time. However, with no notes, it's hard to remember the key points that were discussed.*

The Solution: Failing to listen to prospects is devastating for cold callers, so that's not an option. As a result, use these note-taking guidelines:

Write down anything that will need to be referenced later in the call.

Revisit other key facts in the call recording after the fact as you prepare to handoff the prospect to your salesperson.

Key notes include any of the following:

Metrics: The quantification of something that is or isn't happening that might need to be fixed.

Symptoms of Pain: Signals that pain might exist. These will need to be probed with follow-up questions.

Confirmed Pain Points: Document these points and use them to create urgency for the prospect to show up at the next meeting.

Other Stakeholder Names: Any intel about stakeholders will be valuable to the salesperson if the lead is passed to them.

Going into a calling session, it's key to know what you're looking for to write down. Make your own list using figure 42.1.

Category	What to Understand

Figure 42.1: Key areas for live notes on your calls.

Additional notes for the CRM and to discuss with your salesperson can be jotted down from memory or while listening to the recorded call after the prospect hangs up. Callers who write down *everything* in the moment miss opportunities to ask good questions.

Take Action:

- Revise your note-taking strategy and leverage them on calls for the next week. Review your results and identify additional ways to improve.

SECTION 5: PREPARE FOR FUTURE ROLES

43

YOU AREN'T CONCISE, SPECIFIC, AND ACCURATE

Symptoms:

- You find yourself having to overexplain your points.
- Other people summarize your points using far fewer words than you used to make them.
- Your manager becomes noticeably frustrated in one-on-one conversations.

The Context: Managers, especially senior managers who have been around for a while, have certain expectations when it comes to communication, and these expectations almost always account for the conciseness, specificity, and accuracy of how a person communicates. Poor communication leads to frustrating working relationships and can also lead to a lack of trust, which will ultimately negatively impact a cold caller's performance.

The Solution: Let's review good and bad examples of being concise, specific, and accurate.

Be Concise

Manager: *What's your plan for today?*

Caller: Yeah, I think that I'm going to probably be able to make 100 dials today. I have a quick thing I need to run out for during the middle of the day, but it shouldn't take that long. Then, I think we have the team meeting at 3:00 p.m., or is it 3:30? Anyways, I'll go to that. I've had some real success with the West Coast recently, so I'll probably start calling out there right when they open for business, and might even stay a little late if I'm having success. That seems like about it for today.

Was that statement as painful for you to read as it was for us to write? People get a reputation for being difficult to interact with if every conversation is long and drawn out with excessive narrative. Instead, a concise way of stating the above would be as follows:

Manager: What's your plan for today?

Caller: I'm going to make 100 dials, focusing on the West Coast as soon as I can since I've seen recent success there. Might even work a little late since I need to step out for something personal midday and we have our team meeting at 3:30.

If you're able to be concise, you can cover more ground in the amount of time than if you had been verbose. By covering more ground, you can then get more done both for yourself, as well as for your manager, prospects, and other stakeholders you interact with over time.

Be Specific

Manager: How's it going this week?

Caller: Not good.

Manager: What's wrong?

Caller: We need to rework our messaging. I'm really struggling. Can we do a workshop tomorrow and get messaging figured out?

Manager: *What messaging isn't working? Any of it?*

Caller: *No, just what I'm using for our upcoming webinar.*

Manager: *And it's not working at all?*

Caller: *Not with our finance vertical. That's the only group I've tried it on. I've connected with 15 people and haven't had one person express interest yet.*

The manager in the above example had to pull the specific truth out of the salesperson. A less savvy manager might have taken the caller's words at face value and started to workshop messaging without first figuring out what was going on.

Let's look at the same situation with a more mature caller who is able to outline specifics out of the gate.

Manager: *How's it going this week?*

Caller: *Not good.*

Manager: *What's wrong?*

Caller: *I'm struggling with messaging for our finance vertical. I've had 15 conversations and none of them have converted. I'm going to try another vertical, but if it doesn't work there, we might need to workshop the messaging.*

Manager: *Sounds good. Keep me posted.*

This type of communication style ensures that management can truly understand what's going on.

Be Accurate

> *Manager: How is the new messaging working out?*
>
> *Caller: It's not. I think we need to go back to what we were doing before.*
>
> *Manager: What's happening?*
>
> *Caller: I've called a ton of people and haven't converted one.*
>
> *Manager: How many dials have you made?*
>
> *Caller: Probably 350.*
>
> *Manager: And how many connections?*
>
> *Caller: At least 30.*
>
> *Manager: This week? With the new messaging?*
>
> *Caller: Yeah.*
>
> *Manager: Can you open up the CRM and show me who these folks are so we can dig in deeper?*
>
> *Caller (Opening CRM): Oh, wait. It looks like I've only had seven connects with the new messaging.*
>
> *Manager: On 90 dials, it looks like.*
>
> *Caller: Yeah, sorry. I must have exaggerated a little.*

Exaggerating activity levels and results is somewhat common in the cold calling community, and it's flat-out dangerous. From the company's perspective, they might take these exaggerations at face value and make premature shifts in strategy. From the caller's perspective, if they get a reputation for exaggerating, it can be detrimental to their career.

Take Action:

- Pay attention to the conciseness, specificity, and accuracy of your communication. Tighten it up as needed.

44

YOU USE THE "HOOK ME UP" TACTIC EXTERNALLY

Thanks to sales enablement legend Paul Butterfield for highlighting the pervasive use of the massively ineffective "hook me up" tactic.

Symptoms:

- You ask prospects to take meetings to help you hit your goals even though you know they aren't a good prospect.

The Context:

Cold Caller: *I know that you're not ready to buy now, but I'm trying to hit my quota this quarter, and it would mean a lot if you took a meeting to learn more about our product.*

Yes, your job is to schedule meetings. However, the real goal is to schedule meetings with prospects who are positioned to buy, not with people who have no reason to enter a sales process and want to do you a favor. Imagine what happens to someone's career path when they abandon a focus on sales skills development and beg prospects to do them a favor?

Closing Salesperson: *I really need to hit my quota this quarter. I'll give you a 25% discount if you sign by the end of the month.*

Prospect: *Can't do it.*

Closing Salesperson: *Come on. I really need to hit my quota. How about a 35% discount plus I'll send you some swag? Hook me up.*

Bad habits that are developed as a cold caller will be hard to break and can stick with you over the course of your career.

The Solution: Don't use the "hook me up" close. Instead, identify an acute pain point that they have and your product or service can solve; then put a meeting on the calendar for your prospect and salesperson to discuss.

Take Action:

- Focus on identifying prospect pain and using that to drive them to take a meeting with a salesperson. Avoid asking for them to take the meeting simply as a favor to you.

45

YOU USE THE "HOOK ME UP" CLOSE INTERNALLY

Symptoms:

- You ask salespeople to take meetings with unqualified prospects to help you hit your quota.

The Context: While the external "hook me up" close is less common for cold callers, the internal "hook me up" close is rampant inside many companies.

> *Cold Caller*: *Can you please accept AlphaCorp as an opportunity this month?*

> *Closing Salesperson*: *There's no deal there.*

> *Cold Caller*: *I'm not getting promoted if I don't hit my quota this month. Can you hook me up?*

At this point, the salesperson can either decline or accept the request.

If the lead is accepted, it inflates the company's sales pipeline, meaning that management is making decisions based on numbers that are inaccurate. Furthermore, the cold caller is learning that unethical practices pay off.

In many organizations, cold callers support multiple closers and politics are rampant, so if the closer refuses to accept the opportunity, then there's a chance the cold caller will focus efforts on developing leads for other salespeople.

The Solution: Don't use the "hook me up" close. Instead, rely on the other fundamental skills outlined in this book.

Take Action:

- Simply put, just don't use this tactic. It cheapens your work and hurts your internal brand, and the use of unethical tactics like these will eventually catch up with you and derail your career.

46

YOU MISS OPPORTUNITIES TO PRACTICE SALES SKILLS

Symptoms:

- You have not identified the specific skills you will need in future roles.
- You are not actively practicing skills that will be needed in future roles today, even if they are not necessary to achieve today's goals.

The Context: Many people in cold calling roles today want to move into closing roles in the future. The challenge that folks often run into is that managers hiring for closing roles want people who have closing experience. The good news is that many of the skills needed to be good at closing sales can be practiced on a cold call.

The Solution: Think about the following skills and how they can be applied in a cold calling role:

Pain-Based Discovery Questions: Uncovering a single pain point during a cold call is the most compelling way to get a prospect to show up to the discovery call with the salesperson.

Customer Stories: Telling a customer story is a form of social proof that can be used to help uncover pain or manage Resistance (especially skepticism).

Resistance Management (Objections): Mastering how to manage Resistance is a skill critical to succeeding throughout the entire sales process and can be practiced during the cold call.

Competitive Positioning: The ability to talk professionally about competitors is a key skill from the cold call all the way through the close of a new deal.

Creating Velocity: During any conversation, it's key to create velocity to the next meeting. Cold callers can use this technique to increase the percentage of discovery meetings that hold with their salespeople.

Business Acumen: The more a cold caller knows about a prospect's business, the better their questions will be. Great questions demonstrate Likeness (S.C.A.L.E. framework, chapter 3) and thereby build rapport.

Persona-Based Messaging: Great cold calling requires that messaging throughout the call is highly relevant to the persona of the individual being called. This skill will be used constantly in a closing sales role as well.

These are some of the specific skills needed to find success in a cold calling role, and they are prerequisites for a closing role. Developing these skills makes it easy for management to sign off on a promotion, as they know that the individual is ready to perform as a closer.

Take Action:

- Make a list of skills that are needed to be successful in your next role and figure out how you can use them today.

SECTION 6: MOVING FORWARD

47

PERFORMANCE
IMPROVEMENT ACTIVITIES

At this point we will stop focusing on what people do wrong and suggest some ideas to solve for these issues beyond what we have outlined in each chapter. The good news is that at this point you have a pretty good idea of what to do after having explored countless mistakes made by others.

This chapter focuses on activities that a team can roll out to improve cold calling performance. As an individual contributor, you can step up and be a leader by adopting some of these activities yourself or by introducing them to your team.

These tools will also help your team to facilitate their own enablement instead of leaning on expensive external trainers, who come and go with limited lasting impact.

Negative Goals

Cold callers receive constant rejection, where even a 2% success rate can be considered excellent. Who in the world can feel good about being rejected 98% of the time? Can you imagine that being a positive experience? One way to help your team cope with constant rejection is to focus on "negative goals."

We first talked about the concept of negative goals in *The Sales Enablement Playbook* and have included an excerpt here (excerpt 47.1).

Excerpt 47.1: Negative goals.

Imagine that a cold caller on your team needs to find 50 qualified leads per quarter (roughly four per week). Depending on your business, they might need to communicate with 2,500 people to get to this goal. That means that for every one win there are 49 losses…feels pretty terrible, eh? Here's where negative goals come in:

- Flip the goal from getting 1 yes to getting 49 no's.
- Each time the prospect says no, that's progress toward the goal, not a kick in the teeth.
- Eventually, someone will say yes as well, which is a HUGE win.

Regardless, the cold caller is ALWAYS winning…something.

While it's critical to stay competitive and not be OK with losing, if losing is the norm 90+ percent of the time, companies need to find a way to keep morale strong. Earning a "point" each time someone says no helps people keep pushing instead of getting dejected.

Some people will be able to tough it out through constant rejection, but often it takes a little more. Try negative goals…there's a good chance that your team will be able to push themselves harder than you thought.

Power Hour

The cold calling power hour is a sprint where everyone on the team focuses 100% on dialing for an hour. At the end of the hour, everyone on the team reports back on the number of dials, connects, scheduled meetings, and disqualifications.

Power hours are a way to inject energy and motivation into a team. Some teams will run them multiple times a day, while others have them less frequently if calling is only one of their prospecting channels.

Call Feedback

As we discussed in chapter 14, listening to recorded calls is one of the best ways to improve performance. Doing so in a team setting is even better. To make a team call listening session effective, here are some guidelines:

Establish a "Learning Environment": Have everyone opt in to the fact that they are OK learning from their peers and that they want to collaborate around how to get better. Some use the phrase "safe space" to describe the fact that it's OK to give direct feedback without folks getting upset.

Use a Rubric: Define the categories of feedback and a way to easily capture if you "didn't do it," "did it," or "did it well." An example is shown in figure 14.1 in chapter 14.

Provide Positive and Negative Feedback: Positive feedback helps others realize what to do, while negative feedback corrects poor practice. Make sure that all feedback is in the spirit of learning.

Source the Feedback across the Team: Let everyone participate in giving and receiving feedback. Folks often learn as much or more as they give feedback, as this activity forces them to leverage analytical skills.

Tie All Feedback to Rubric: All feedback should be routed in the rubric. If holes in the rubric are found, adjust the rubric. Once feedback goes outside the bounds of the rubric, then it becomes more of an ad hoc opinion, which isn't as useful.

As you can see, having a common language in the form of a rubric is critical for any team feedback session. An example is provided in figure 47.2.

Component	Cold Caller		Manager	
	Score	Notes	Score	Notes
Intro	1		1	
P.L.A.N.	1		0	Did not complete
Elevator Pitch	2	I think I nailed it	2	Highly relevant!
Pain	1		2	Very strong!
Resistance	2		2	Solid technique
Next Steps	1		1	
Rapport	1		1	
Questions	1	Felt like I could have improved	1	Let's discuss; opportunity here

Figure 47.2: Cold call rubric (from chapter 14).

Team Dialing

Team dialing involves two people sitting in a room together and taking turns making dials. On the surface, this format is twice as expensive to the organization, but when done in moderation, it provides for a great motivational and teamwork-oriented experience.

The learning that comes from experiencing a teammate's style and observing how they manage rejection is a good way to inject some energy into the cold calling culture.

Role Play Breaks

Putting role plays on the calendar gives cold callers something to look forward to, while also giving them the opportunity to practice their craft with peers. Role plays often fit into the "important but not urgent" category of activities, so they don't happen, at least not as much as they should, if they're not put on the calendar. We covered some specifics on this topic in chapter 38.

Take Action:

- Make a list of activities you will start making part of your daily, weekly, and monthly workflow, and put them into action!

48

GETTING STARTED

At this point, you should have either validated that everything you're doing today is spot-on or have identified some areas for improvement. Now it's time to make some calls while rolling out what you have learned from this book.

If you have a list of things you need to change but don't know where to start, try plotting them on the effort vs. impact 2 x 2 matrix in figure 48.1.

Figure 48.1: Map priorities across effort and impact.

Once it's clear where to start, create a lightweight project management plan for yourself, as shown in figure 48.2.

Task	Completion Date	Signs of Success
Create Rubric	This week	My manager & I both score 3 calls per week.
Create Call Framework	Next week	My conversion rates increase by 5% next month.
Conduct 5 Role Plays	This month	I don't lose my cool during real life calls.

Figure 48.2: Lightweight project management plan.

We (probably) don't know you. We also don't know your long-term goals in life. However, if you're like many cold callers we have met over the years, you want to get better at what you do today, and you want to leverage these skills to get promoted into other roles. Throughout this book we have provided the diagnostic tools to identify where your current efforts might be lacking, as well as some ideas on how to improve.

Furthermore, we are pushing you to become a better *business person* instead of just saying "make more dials," "20x your efforts," or some other motivational slogan that has no depth. Diagnosing challenges? Creating a 2 x 2 matrix? Putting together and running a project plan? These are skills critical for success in business, especially management, and unfortunately most folks in cold calling roles are not able to get exposure to this type of work in their day-to-day jobs. That's where this book can give you a leg up on your peers who are focused on listening to motivational speakers at conferences or on LinkedIn; they give you enough to get a "like" but not enough to move the needle on your career.

You might have noticed that there was no mention of creating a personal brand in this book. There is an endless supply of online personalities who steer folks to investing countless hours to create a personal brand. Upon further inspection, people often find that their personal branding efforts do more to help the "create a brand like me" gurus expand their reach than it does to help cold callers achieve their professional goals of booking meetings and building their skill set. Social selling has its place. Personal branding has its place. However, if your goal is to achieve success in a cold calling role, we advise that you first and foremost focus on achieving mastery across the fundamental skills outlined in this book. That's what will lead to quota overachievement and a rapid promotion path to the job of your dreams. Employers want to hire and promote winners, and your ability to master your craft is the number one way you can demonstrate your ability to win.

If you like what you've read in these pages and want to learn more about how we help folks like you, head on over to ColdCallBook.com for additional resources. And remember, never deliver a message without a call-to-action at the end!